In the Arena

MIKE CURRY

Fulton Books, Inc.
Meadville, PA

Published by Fulton Books 2020

ISBN 978-1-64654-046-4 (paperback)
ISBN 978-1-64654-614-5 (digital)

Printed in the United States of America

It is not the critic who counts; not the man who points out how the strong man stumbles, or where the doer of deeds could have done them better. The credit belongs to the man who is actually in the arena, whose face is marred by dust and sweat and blood; who strives valiantly; who errs, who comes short again and again; who spends himself in a worthy cause; who at the best knows in the end the triumph of high achievement, and who at the worst, if he fails, at least fails while daring greatly, so that his place shall never be with those cold and timid souls who neither know victory nor defeat.

—Theodore Roosevelt
April 23, 1910

Foreword

The genesis for this project came from some writings of my wife's grandmother passed down through her family. The writings describe a time none of us had or would experience and a much younger person than we would have known.

I know almost nothing about the lives of my parents or grandparents. Unfortunately, as a general rule, when we die the texture of our lives is lost. I have had some great experiences, and I wanted to leave something behind that allowed other generations to know something about me.

Initially, I wrote about my experience as a Marine Corps infantry officer in Vietnam. My writing was based on official Marine Corps records and numerous letters I wrote home. Then I expanded that to include incidents noted in diary entries from my rather tumultuous years in education. I added the Watts Riots and the years I spent in Jamaica as a Peace Corps volunteer. The latter also based on letters.

I have changed the name of the schools as well as both teachers and students, or I didn't use a name. It seemed a prudent thing to do. Many of these incidents are not in chronological order. I grouped some of them in order to provide some sense of order, particularly if it involved the same student or group of students. Also, these incidents took place over a thirty-one-year span and in two different schools. However incredible, I made nothing up. It all happened.

Some of the incidents I describe are trivial in the larger scale of things and some are not. Most, literally thousands of students who attended Jefferson Middle School and Franklin Elementary, have gone on to become productive citizens. Numerous positive things went on in the school, thanks to some wonderful teachers. However, most situations I describe are not positive because they represent where I spent so much of my time. As with countless other situations, it is the problems, the exceptions to the norm, that suck the air out of the room. In some cases, they were traumatic incidents. My account also gives the reader an idea of the constant barrage and diversity of issues occurring in a school.

1

The Beginning

We were just wrapping up the conference when she reached for her pistol. *Whoa!* My teacher emitted an audible gasp and clearly looked faint. I, for a change, was rendered speechless. To say this turn of events was unexpected would be a classic understatement. I thought the conference had gone well, it had been low keyed and non confrontational.

As a member of the California National Guard patrolling Central Avenue during the 1965 Watts Riots, I watched fires light up the Los Angeles skyline. While a Peace Corps volunteer, I coped with many unpredictable and unexpected situations. I even had been shot at in Vietnam while a Marine Corps infantry officer leading long-range reconnaissance teams. But I never actually had a gun pulled on me. A knife, yes. A gun, no.

Fortunately for everybody involved, the parent, waving her gun, said she brought the gun to insure we took her seriously. I can absolutely and unequivocally assure you we were taking her very seriously! Saying that, she put the gun back into her purse, got up, and left.

My teacher made a beeline for the exit in the opposite direction. He no doubt thought we were about to be shot. He was taking no chances she might come back with her gun. Subsequently, he requested a transfer saying he thought it too dangerous in this school.

Well, admittedly, a parent with a gun did qualify under the too-dangerous label. However, with that big exception, the school was not too dangerous. It was an inner-city school filled with all kinds of challenging situations during a difficult period of our history: desegregation. Birmingham City Schools were operating under court-ordered desegregation that resulted in some pretty intense situations. Middle schools were created to facilitate the court order.

How was it that I participated in some major historical events of my time? More immediately, how did I end up as a middle school principal with a woman waving her gun in my face?

Well, that is my story. It is the story I am sharing with you. It starts as far back as first grade.

"I don't want to go to school!"

"Me neither!"

"Let's ditch."

"Okay."

"Wanna ride horses?"

So the conversation went, walking to school in first grade. Well, Gary was in kindergarten, but at that age, easily influenced.

Off we went to Mission Valley. At that time, Mission Valley was an undeveloped area filled with ponds, quicksand, and horse pastures several miles from where we lived.

Our parents never would have allowed us in the area. It was no secret kids sometimes drowned there.

We had to navigate thick brush, snake-filled canyons, cross a small two-lane road, and climb over various fences to get to the horse pastures. Too small to mount the horses, we climbed the fence and jumped on the back of any horse standing next to it. We were having a great time!

That all came to a screeching halt when the police showed up! We were bundled into the police car and hauled off to the school principal's office. The dreaded principal's office. Little did I know then what the future had in store for me.

That pretty much set the tone for my early academic endeavors. My mother met with a teacher or the principal virtually every year I was in school.

My father, the oldest of seven children, met my mother at a fraternity mixer his freshman year at San Diego State University, a teachers college at that time. He was a big guy who played football and belonged to Sigma Chi fraternity. She was a small woman who was a member of Alpha Gamma Delta sorority. At least as far as he was concerned, it was love at first sight. He and my mother dropped out of college and got married. My father started work as a tinsmith at the Naval Air Station at North Island and worked his way up the hierarchy.

I was born January 27, 1942. World War II was well underway. The government discouraged workers at North Island from joining the Armed Forces because their work was judged to be too valuable to the war effort. Both my father's brothers served: Bob as a decorated Navy fighter pilot off a carrier and in many battles in the Pacific, and Keith in the United States Marine Corps. Keith was among the first Marines to land in Japan after the atomic bomb. Entering the harbor, he saw firsthand the devastation created by American air raids. Had not Japan surrendered, he would have been among the first invading forces with little chance for his survival.

I was incredibly lucky to have good parents. My father was a great role model who set an enviably high standard for us, but because of their service in WWII, Bob and Keith were my heroes. Keith being a Marine had a lot to do with me choosing the Marine Corps. They participated in a seminal event in American history, and sadly, their stories are lost. I never had a really good conversation with either of them about their experiences. They wrote nothing down. I have only a few letters they wrote home and their military records. I don't want that to happen to me.

My mother gave birth to my brother Gary a year after I was born and Paul four years later. She worked part time at various jobs in order to make ends meet. Around Christmas, I remember her working at Sears, Roebuck and Company where she got a discount on our school clothes.

We lived in the house next to my mother's parents until I was in sixth grade then moved to Spring Valley. Living next to my grandparents was both good and bad. My grandfather was a very able craftsman. At Christmas, my parents would buy secondhand toys, and my grandfather would redo them so that they looked brand new.

He also made several boats. One of them was a cabin cruiser he took out to the kelp beds fishing. He liked company, and we were the most likely suspects. Gary and I got roused out of bed at some ungodly hour on weekends. It was pitch black when we left port, and one or both of us would invariably get seasick.

We had one of the first little black-and-white televisions in our neighborhood. My grandfather would regularly come over to watch professional wrestling and roller derby.

The downside of having them next door was that my grandfather was an alcoholic and a mean one at that. My mother carried some resentment, growing up in a house where she was afraid to bring a friend over, not knowing whether or not her father would be sober. My grandmother, whom Dad called Foxy because he said she was always one step ahead of everyone, would frequently check all of his stashes. He went on the wagon for seven years because his doctor told him if he continued to drink, it would kill him. Then one day while my grandmother was away visiting relatives, he fell off the wagon, and he started drinking again. It killed him within a year. His death was hard on our family, but it did bring my grandmother closer to us. I think, at times, my mother struggled with their relationship, but my father and the three of us enjoyed her sense of humor. Even into college, I would bring dates over to her house for her delicious homemade pancakes.

In third grade, I definitely struggled with math. I don't think I was doing red hot with my teacher either. My parents took us out of public school and enrolled us in Saint Didacus, a Catholic school. One year, I was a nun's favorite and the next year, not so much. Sister Mary gave me her personal prayer book and a load of encouragement. Sister Rose gave me the sharp edge of her tongue and hair-raising stories of what the devil did with misbehaving children.

My mother didn't care for the parish priest in Spring Valley, so we went back to public school. My mother's visits to my teachers and/or principal resumed. I was somewhat rebellious and a general pain in the ass to everyone involved. I took exception to whatever anyone in authority might suggest, particularly my parents. I also was the resident expert on most topics.

My wife claims nothing has changed.

Gary and I were a definite trial to my parents. Paul seemed to slip by without ever getting caught. Gary and I constantly got into some kind of mischief, fought each other, or did something really stupid that left one of us hurt. I showed Gary a judo move that knocked him out cold. I thought that I had killed him! On another occasion, we were playing in the canyon as we frequently did, and Gary threw a bamboo spear just as I told him not to. I ended up with a hole next to my eye resulting in the first of many stiches I acquired over the years. If my parents scolded Gary, he likely would go out and start a fire or break a window. If punished, I would run away.

I easily was in more trouble more frequently than either brother, probably because Paul was too young, and Gary figured out that whenever he did something wrong, he got caught. I was much slower to work that out.

Running away as a strategy, didn't work out well for me. My mother would help me pack my suitcase and send me off. I would sit down in the canyon for the day, get hungry, and trudge back home, thoroughly chastened.

We were a family of ice cream-a-holics. My father even owned an ice cream shop at one point. The three of us fought a nightly running battle over who would dish out the ice cream; each of us claiming that whoever did ended up with the biggest bowl. My father, demonstrating the wisdom of Solomon, decreed that whomever dished out the ice cream got the last bowl chosen. The result was bowls so evenly divided it would have made a weights and measurement expert proud.

In San Diego, we lived in a small, two-bedroom house. The three of us slept in the same room. Gary and I had bunk beds. Nightly, we would giggle and carry on despite numerous threats and warnings from our parents. Finally, my dad would have enough and off would come his belt. Gary got the worst of it because he was on the bottom bunk well within the belt's reach. On the top bunk, I would roll next to the wall where the belt barely reached and yell bloody murder. Paul had enough sense to lay low, thereby escaping the belt.

We moved to Spring Valley when I was twelve. Spring Valley at that time still had avocado and orange orchards. There were not a whole lot of houses around us. Behind our house was a hillside full of brush, small wild animals, and snakes. We wandered everywhere with little parental supervision. I met my best childhood friend and my parent's all-time favorite, David Wagner. David instigated virtually all the adventures and good times I had growing up. My parents even included him on our family vacations.

One of my mom's fondest stories was waking up on a weekend morning and finding David sitting in our living room patiently waiting for us to get up and fix breakfast. He liked my mom's waffles. In those days, no one locked their house or closed the garage door.

One of my best memories involved his junior high girlfriend. She would ride her horse over to visit David. They would sit on the rim of a canyon. While they canoodled, I would ride the horse. It worked out well for all involved.

Once we got our driver's license, we would go surfing, or occasionally, with Gary, take our .22 rifles and head out to a shack on the Yuma River. We would hunt rabbits, skinny dip in the river, and tell ghost stories. Ghost stories, vivid imaginations, the rustling of bushes as the nighttime wind blew would have us prowling around our abandoned shack rifles in hand. It was a small miracle we didn't shoot each other.

One night in the summer, Gary, David, and I decided to camp out on the beach. We fortified ourselves with a couple of bottles of Thunderbird and Ripple (cheap wine that we conned someone into buying for us). We built a fire. After dark, we went surfing in the buff. Sitting on our surfboards, we began talking about sharks and what part of our anatomy they might nibble on. We headed back to the beach while we had all parts intact.

After more Ripple and Thunderbird, I got the sickest I can ever remember being. I could not even lift my head, much less crawl into my sleeping bag. It marked the end of any more Ripple or Thunderbird adventures.

High school was good. Although a very indifferent student, I somehow got included in a group of excellent students. Several had swimming pools that made for some really good parties. I played football and wrestled in high school with limited success. My senior year, the year that should have been my year, I got hurt playing both sports. It prematurely ended my high school athletic career. The real athletic success in the family was my younger brother Paul. He was a terrific wrestler on a nationally recognized high school wrestling team. He could have been a scholarship athlete in college but chose to concentrate on academics. Okay, well, there may have been some partying in there, too, but I think Paul's United States Marine Corps boot camp experience clarified his priorities as far as college went. Both Gary, who also wrestled in high school, and I played a little rugby in college. Gary played at the University of Oregon.

My mother continued her visits with one teacher or another due to my conduct or lack of academic endeavor. I managed to intercept a mailed report card and change the grades, only a very short-term solution. Another time, she came home to find the truant officer waiting on our front steps. Probably the highlight came when she received a call from my chemistry teacher right before graduation, informing her that I was failing chemistry and would not graduate. It took some negotiation with the chemistry teacher to slide out of that fix. In my defense, all the really good-looking girls were in my chemistry class. I thought my time much better spent chatting them up than doing any of my work.

Needless to say, when it came time to go to college, I couldn't find any four-year school that would accept me. Consequently, I enrolled in San Diego City College, a two-year school. I spent a year there, then transferred to Grossmont College followed by San Diego State University.

I enrolled at San Diego State midterm, went through rush, and joined Tau Kappa Epsilon fraternity. I thoroughly enjoyed college, which is probably why I spent four years at what should have been done in two. I carried a full academic load while working nearly full time at various jobs. My academic record remained less than stellar. My senior year I got a job that left my afternoons free, so I was able to join the rugby team at San Diego State. That began a lifelong love of rugby.

Kenny Jones, a fraternity brother, and I both were on academic probation. We got a wild hair to join the Coast Guard. There were no openings in San Diego, so we hitch-hiked to Phoenix, Arizona, to join up. We got there on the weekend, so if they had an opening, we wouldn't have known because they were closed. Of course, Phoenix seems an unlikely place for the Coast Guard, and we certainly didn't check it out beforehand. With that sort of planning, it was no mystery as to why we were on academic probation.

As it turned out, we joined the California National Guard along with fifty other students from San Diego State. The only time I saw my dad tear up was when I told him I was dropping out of school to go to basic training at Fort Ord. He had put his hopes in me being the first in the family to graduate from college despite my dismal academic record. Of course, in my perpetual hubris, I knew I would return to school, and his emotions were unfounded. The irony of my relationship with my dad is that I wanted to please him, and yet, I continually did things that upset him.

What I remember most about basic training was I always seemed to get KP (kitchen police) or guard duty while Kenny always managed to find a way to get out of it. He never missed the opportunity to rub it in either. I would be outside, scrubbing pots and pans, and he would be at a window of the squad bay, whistling and waving. Well, actually, I also remember the Army giving us a class on brushing our teeth. Of course, after visiting the dentist as part of our induction physical, many recruits had fewer teeth.

Jones and I survived basic training, returned to school, got off probation, and actually graduated from college, no doubt shocking everyone involved.

In 1968, I was helping my roommate and surfing buddy, Claude Lubin, as he painted some of the apartments in our complex. From the second floor, he dropped an open roller pan of paint for me to catch. I knew that was not going to work out well, and I took off running. The pan hit the ground, and the paint reached out and covered me head to foot.

On the ground floor, standing with her suitcases next to all this paint splatter and slapstick comedy, was a young lady just moving in to the apartments. Fortunately, none of the paint got on her or her luggage. I wasted no time in striking up a conversation with this attractive young lady who had beautiful long auburn hair. The paint splatter provided the icebreaker. Her name was Carol Cords. She grew up in Ocean Beach, attended the University of Arizona for a year, and currently was working at Sea World, saving money to enroll at San Diego State.

Had the paint gotten on her or her luggage, history might have been changed. As it turned out, Carol Cords became my wife and the mother of my children.

I signed up with a group of high school boys during the summer to pick pineapples for the Maui Pineapple Company in Maui, Hawaii. I was to supervise a group of pickers in the field as well as the boys in our sleeping quarters. The sleeping quarters consisted of a large room, part of a local elementary school in Lahaina, a small town on the coast. I was thoroughly entertained, lying in bed, listening to teenage boys interact with each other. The teasing and pranks were constant and at times quite clever. One boy, a favorite target of the others, drew a very detailed figure of a naked woman on his bottom bed sheet. He found his sheet missing one day. The boys told him they had mailed it to his father, a minister.

We all showed up with our surfboards, intending to spend our time waxing our boards, working on our tans, and surfing. Actual work was an afterthought, so it came as shock to find out we were expected to work six days a week and eight-plus hours a day in the heat, picking pineapples. We were divided into shifts and teams and assigned jobs. The best job as far as the boys were concerned was driving one of the monstrous trucks carrying pineapples from the fields to the sheds. The most arduous job was moving down the rows, picking pineapples. A day in the fields exhausted us and definitely impinged on our surfing time.

Much to my parents' relief, I graduated from San Diego State University.
Seen here with my mother, my father and "Foxy," my grandmother.

The Curry brothers: Paul, Mike and Gary, no doubt contemplating many
weighty matters… "Do you think Dad has any more beer in the refridge?"

Many Maui residents, far more accustomed to the heat and hard work, also picked pineapples. They lived in areas referred to as camps that seemed to be identified by their ethnic origin (e.g., Philippine Camp, Japanese Camp, and Hawaiian Camp). They came to the fields with their lunches in small two-part cylindrical cans. The bottom portion held rice, and the top portion had their fish or vegetables. I found it all interesting and exotic. Their lunches looked far more appetizing than ours.

After work, we gathered up our surfboards and headed out for Lahaina. We surfed off a jetty next to the small town. This very picturesque setting had few tourists and maybe one hotel. Maui had not yet been discovered by the tourist industry. It paid to be a proficient surfer because the surf broke over coral, and you could get pretty cut up with a few mishaps off the board. I swapped out my board for a much better one and got to be a fairly decent surfer.

I was a big fan of James Michener's book, *Hawaii*. I envisioned getting married in one of the scenic little churches described by Michener. Well, that turned out to be a pipe dream. In August 1968, Red met me upon my return, and we decided on a very small wedding. With about three days' notice, we called our parents. My parents were excited. Her mother was decidedly less so. However, we persevered.

2

Watts Riots 1965

August 1965

I hate climbing telephone poles. Twenty feet up may not seem that high, but for someone with a fear of heights, it looks like a very long way down. The Army designated me as a telephone communication crewman. That meant learning to climb telephone poles. Predictably, it did not turn out well.

We trainees were issued gaffs that helped us climb the poles. The gaffs were not curved, so if I got too close to the pole, the gaffs would come out of the pole and down I would go. Safety belts, certainly an oxymoron in my case, were not hooked on until the climber was situated at the top of the pole.

The poles, used by many trainees, were filled with splinters from previous climbers' gaffs. My anxiety rose, looking down from the top of the pole. Foolishly, I took off my gloves to get a better purchase while trying to hook on my safety belt. My gaffs gave out and down I went, safety belt dangling! Clinging to the pole, it was a horrifying descent. I could feel chunks of wood breaking off in my hands as I plunged downward. My hands looked like wood-filled hamburger. I immediately became the center of attention, standing with bloody hands in the middle of the sandpit where the poles were located. The pain in my hands was compounded by the utter humiliation I felt for letting it happen in the first place. The medic bandaged me up and saw me off to the hospital where they removed most of the splinters. That ended any pole climbing. I went back to my unit and volunteered to be a scout driver.

On August 13, 1965, we reported to our armory for our two-week annual training (AT). We were scheduled to go to Fort Irwin. I was a member of the California National Guard's 40th Armored Division.

The riots in Los Angeles started a day or two before we left for our annual training. The spark that set the riots off resulted from an escalation of a traffic stop by the police of a black motorist for reckless driving. Some National Guard units had just been activated to help the police. We were in a convoy on our way to Fort Irwin when word came down that we were activated. We were redirected to Los Angeles. We could see the LA skyline lighted up with the flames of burning businesses. Everyone was pretty excited about the prospect of a new adventure. The reality of the tragedy occurring was lost on us. It just seemed better than two boring weeks at Fort Irwin. Ultimately, nearly four thousand National Guard troops were activated for the riots.

On the third day of the riot, our unit was bivouacked in the parking area of a racetrack. It was late afternoon when we got set up, and from there various patrols were sent out. I didn't spend any time there that I can remember. Eager to get involved with whatever I could, I volunteered immediately for whatever came up. That mostly entailed cordoning off streets and enforcing an 8 p.m. curfew. Whatever we were assigned, I wanted to be right in the middle of what was going on. No doubt it was the same compulsion that led me to becoming an infantry officer, leading long-range reconnaissance teams in Vietnam rather than choosing something a little safer.

The National Guard was in no way prepared for anything, especially riot duty. There is a story, perhaps apocryphal, about a couple of guardsmen guarding our bivouac area one night. One soldier was carrying an automatic weapon with which he was not altogether familiar. They were chatting with each other, he was fiddling with his weapon, and it went off. Across the street, a drive-in theater was showing a cowboy movie. As the cowboys' horses raced from one side of the screen to the other, little holes in the screen appeared to be chasing them. Fortunately, with all the shooting in the movie, no one took note of a few extra rounds being discharged.

Another story reflecting the National Guard's struggle with competence occurred as troops were being dropped off on Central Avenue. The press wanted a visual so they set up the filming of a sergeant coming off a truck with others to secure an intersection. The sergeant leaped from the truck, pulled out his .45 caliber pistol, attempted to chamber a round, and in the process, got the pistol all jammed up. The guard issued each rifleman two rounds of ammunition. Officers and NCOs got more. Not good for the visual, so they put him back on the truck to do it over. This time, when he dramatically pulled his pistol, it accidentally went off. Well, that was too much for all involved, so they took all of his bullets away and put him back on the truck. He missed his fifteen minutes of fame. Later at our annual training, he drove his tank into a ditch. It had to be towed out. All in all, he had a pretty rough two weeks.

I was put on a deuce-and-a-half truck (2 1/2 ton) with a bunch of other guardsmen. We were taken to Central Ave., the main street flowing through Watts, and dropped off on each corner. Our job was to cordon off Central Ave. Virtually every store within sight had been burned and looted. Detritus from the looting and burning was everywhere. Liquor stores got lots of attention from the looters. The number of drunken people I encountered was impressive, to say nothing of the language I couldn't remotely decipher.

I was dropped off on an intersection with a guy I did not know. He was carrying a submachine gun neither of us knew how to work. In other words, we had no clue how to put the gun on safe. As I remember, this guy was a spindly little guy with military issue glasses and a big helmet on a small head. His appearance did not inspire confidence.

But he outranked me. "Curry," he said. "You get out and stop any oncoming traffic. I will be right behind you. If the car doesn't stop, just drop to your knees, and I'll fire over your head."

Now that really did not sound like a good plan to me! I had absolutely zero confidence in him and no intention of being anywhere near where he pointed his gun. Fortunately, we never had to test it.

One incident stood out in my mind. Our job was to cordon off the street. No cars were allowed. When a car came, weaving down the street, we stopped it. The driver was drunk as a coot. I had absolutely no idea of what he was trying to say in answer to any of my questions. His mumbled answers were incoherent. It was a frustrating few minutes. We were trying to tell him he could not be on that street. As previously instructed when any situation arose, we notified the police. They came and got him, leaving his car there on the street. Hours later, when the police returned him to his car, he looked like he had taken a real beating. He seemed to be missing a few front teeth. I felt guilty for calling the police and pretty much decided from that point to not call the police for any more drunk stops.

During the day, it was well over a hundred degrees. Hot! The street was lined with what seemed to be second-story apartments. All the windows to the upstairs apartments were open. People were sitting at their open windows in order to get the benefit of any draft. Many were fanning themselves to encourage some air movement. We could see those at the windows but not further back in the apartment. We could hear someone we couldn't see in the window rhythmically cocking a gun, maybe a BB gun, and pulling the trigger. Against a backdrop of a burning city and hearing the occasional gunfire, that sound gave us some anxiety. I think for the most part, residents were happy for us to be on the street. We provided them a sense of security from the chaos of the riot. They occasionally offered some much appreciated courtesies.

For example, the next hot, miserable day, a little black kid dressed in a miniature Army outfit went to each of us bringing cold drinks. It certainly provided a counterpoint to all the drinking and foul language. In the early hours of the morning, exhausted, we lay down on the filthy sidewalk and slept, hoping fervently we would not catch some awful disease.

Eventually, the area was deemed secured, and having returned our two rounds of ammunition, we boarded our trucks for our annual training. Standing in formation at Fort Irwin, a shot rang out from just behind us. We turned and saw an officer with a hole in the bottom of his holster. He rather sheepishly told us we should all check our weapons. It merely confirmed to me that we had some really unqualified people running things.

The riots devastated Watts. There were thirty-four deaths and over $40 million in property damage. Most Watts residents were not burning, breaking into stores, or looting. Many of the stores were not rebuilt. It seemed unfair that those who were not involved were the people who suffered most from the riot.

That seeming incompetence of the National Guard was one reason why I joined the United States Marine Corps when I decided to go to war.

3

Vietnam

September 1968

The Marine Corps recruiter was nonplussed when I showed up at the recruiting station ready to sign up. So many college students were avoiding the military, he had a hard time coming to terms with me wanting to volunteer. Not only was I volunteering, but I virtually had completed my military obligation. He didn't actually say he thought I was crazy, but I have no doubt it crossed his mind. At first, he suggested that I might be better off sticking with the Army since I had close to six years in already. He made sure I knew signing up for the Marine Corps was a sure ticket to Vietnam. "Sign me up!" I was determined to become a Marine Corps infantry officer!

Actually, I tried to join the Marine Corps much earlier in college. A friend, Allen Lochman, and I traveled to the Marine Recruiting Station in Los Angeles for our physicals. Allen wore thick glasses. When he took them off to read the eye chart, he was sunk. I think his words were, "What chart?" The Navy doctors diagnosed me with a curvature of the spine. They felt it would inhibit my Marine Corps training and activities. We both flunked!

Times changed. The Vietnam War consumed more young Marine Corps officers. I persisted, took the tests, signed the papers, and was ready to go. My physical wasn't an issue this time.

I joined the Marine Corps in 1968 despite having served in the California National Guard for over five years. This was a time when getting into the National Guard was a way to get out of going to Vietnam, by now a very unpopular war. However, it didn't seem quite right to me, though I was no big supporter of the war, that I could avoid going to war, and a bunch of drafted eighteen-year-old kids right out of high school wouldn't have that option.

However, time passed, and my orders still did not arrive, so I boarded a plane in San Diego for Washington, D.C. and then got on a train to Quantico, Virginia. Aboard the train, I met a few others headed for Officer Candidate School (OCS). There was an air of excitement among us all.

I struck up a conversation with one guy who was very preppy looking and appeared to have it all together. He said his name was Jack (not his name), he was from Los Angeles, had been in a fraternity in college, and had taught high school biology in Los Angeles. I figured he was a good guy to get to know. We did end up in the same platoon, but things did not run as smoothly for him as he or I thought they would.

Ultimately, we arrived at the Marine Corps Base in Quantico, Virginia. I had no orders or anything other than my suitcase. Casualty figures being what they were, the Marine Corps, feeling a need for more young officers, took me anyway. It was the beginning of what was one of the most satisfying and challenging journeys of my life.

Officer Candidate School

December 2, 1968

If I get my bars here, I will earn them. From what everyone says, it is really going to be hard. So far, we have been harassed plenty. The first night, Monday night, we stayed up until midnight, pushing lockers around, getting dressed and undressed a hundred times or so, and just generally being harassed by the drill instructors. They would get right up in an officer candidate's face, yelling and doing their best to intimidate and fluster the candidate. They were very good at it too.

We got up at 5:30 a.m., and I was plenty tired. Since then, I have been kept busy. Even on Thanksgiving, which we were supposed to have off, the drill instructor kept us busy all day. It seems like I've been here a month or two instead of just a week. The drill instructor storms in every morning, yelling and banging on lockers and trash cans. Startled, we are up and out of bed before we even realize it. The day begins with a rush that doesn't end until we are back in the rack for lights out.

It hasn't snowed here yet, but it does get a bit nippy. I am destitute and need to buy several things, among them thermal underwear. I have had a headache since Thanksgiving. I was really sick on Thanksgiving, but except for a dull pain, haven't felt too bad since.

The clothes I wore here are a sight—wrinkled, torn, and dirty. They told everyone to show up in a good suit! The only catch: we can't leave without a tie on weekends. I bought one at the PX so I could leave if I wanted.

Dec. 3, 1968

Around here, everyone is really sick. At least ten guys in my platoon alone have barfed, and many more had the runs. More are getting sick all the time. I don't know why.

Tomorrow, we really start in on the training. There are guys from all over the country in here. My bunkmate is from Arkansas. Denny Cox is built like a small fireplug. He played football—linebacker, no less—at a small Arkansas college. With all the southerners here, I will probably come home with a southern accent.

Dec. 4, 1968

Boy! My head still hurts, really hurts. Now five days straight.

We ran the obstacle course today. Some of these candidates are very uncoordinated and weak. Jack, the preppy guy I met on the train, is really a nice guy, but without a doubt, the weakest and most uncoordinated person I have ever seen. The drill instructors got on him right away and haven't let up. They told him one more mistake and he goes. That is a pretty scary proposition.

We will have a Christmas leave for sure, and the cadre platoon sergeant told us no one would be allowed to stay here because he and the rest of the staff don't want to have to come in to keep an eye on us. I don't blame them. I wouldn't either.

Some guy stole my field jacket liner right off the bat, so I suppose I will have to pay for it.

Jack is so uncoordinated he has to wear a coat hanger in his shirt to keep his posture straight. He really looks funny. It is amazing how someone can maintain an image in one situation and have it totally shattered in another.

I would like to get some pills for my headache. However, they take all pills, including aspirin away from us. I am enduring.

Dec. 8, 1968

I'm in command voice class right now. It's a real winner! I probably need it. My platoon sergeant told me to practice yelling out of my car window to strengthen my voice. Tomorrow we have an inspection. I've got so many things to do tonight, I don't know where to start. Trouble is, around here, they don't give you enough time to do anything.

I am waiting for a conduct of the march class to start. We have our first hike today. They say the hikes are worse than the runs, and the runs are certainly no fun. I haven't even cleaned my rifle yet. It has rust on it. I hope I get a little time to do that tonight, or it could be bad news.

The drill instructors regularly empty our footlockers on the floor. They found candy in mine the other night. While I was standing at attention in my skivvies in front of my bunk, the drill instructor roundly abused me for having an unauthorized item. He then made me stuff the whole pack of jellybeans into my mouth at once and chew it. I will be more careful in the future. I like jellybeans, but I prefer them one at a time.

It is after lunch now, so the day is almost over by my reckoning. Of course, the hardest part of the day comes at the end when we have physical training (PT) or hikes.

Well, it is Saturday night, and I finally have a chance to finish a letter home. I can't say I did really well Friday on our march. The drill instructor threw me out of the platoon on the hike. That made me a straggler. I was passing a couple of guys in front of me, and he got me for being out of line, just the opposite of straggling. At any rate, I got a chit that says, "You straggled on the hill trail on hike #1. Remember, it is impossible for a man to lead if he is himself running behind." Since a straggling chit is one of the worst you can get, it really ticked me off. I also got one for not signing my autobiography and two for my clothes and bunk, for a grand total of four! Nice going!

We came back into the bay Friday and found everything turned upside down. Just a little more harassment on top of what is already the worst part of this deal—the running. The running really hurts!

We had an inspection this morning, which, of course, we all failed. I had to throw away some hometown newspapers that were sent to me. I didn't even have the time to read them.

We have a two-thousand-word essay to write on military courtesy, for punishment, so I had better sign off and get busy. I also have a test Monday to study for and guard to stand tomorrow.

Dec. 10, 1968

Brother, was it cold today! I have never felt such cold. And we had to spend the whole day outside! We took a test Monday, and I barely passed. Today, we had camouflage and concealment. In the afternoon, we had bayonet and physical training. Some guy got carried away in an ambulance. He got hit in the ribs with a knee or something. Anyway, his ribs were hurt. They're starting to drop like flies around here. Three guys have been physically disqualified from my platoon alone. The preppy guy who was so uncoordinated and wore a coat hanger may have a detached retina. He sat down in class and poked himself in the eye with the rifle of the guy seated in front of him. Another guy took off for the weekend. No one has seen him since.

Wow! It is now Wednesday night, and I have two more chits. I got caught sleeping in class and had to hold a footlocker against my chest while partially bent over. I also straggled on a run. That is very bad.

Dec. 12, 1968

I am really tired and can't wait to go to bed. We wake up every morning by jumping out of bed with our sheets in both hands and a pillowcase in our mouth. Then we run downstairs, line up on the pavement outside, and do some exercises. We run back upstairs, hit the head (bathroom), shave, make our beds, and then get ready for the day. All this is done in about thirty minutes. We then fall out again on the pavement to march off to chow and our classes.

After classes and drill and harassment, we spend about an hour doing physical training. It is a real killer too! Everyone dreads it. I sure hope I hurry up and get in better shape. We sleep in an open bay room filled with rows of bunk beds. At night, every night, we all stand in front of our bunks in our issued white boxer shorts and T-shirt and count off in order to make sure everyone is there. After counting off, we sing the *Marine Corps Hymn*. The drill instructor then says, "Prepare to mount!" We get by the side of our bunks. He says, "Mount!" We then jump on top of our bunks, yelling, "Gung Ho!" We lay there at attention until he says, "Get in and sleep." Going to sleep is the easy part!

Tomorrow, we start "billets," which means we run ourselves, and we are graded on our actions. Here is where it gets tough.

Today, Thursday, we went through the reaction course. I did okay, I guess. They give us a leadership grade for it. It rained like the devil yesterday, and we got soaked. The weather has definitely gotten nippy. I'm going to get some thermal underwear.

Dec. 15, 1968

We went on our second training hike Thursday. Our hikes always include the dreaded hill trail, a particularly arduous piece of terrain, and a part of OCS lore. I survived with flying colors and a corn on my toe. In the process, I picked up a sore throat though. We came back from lunch before the hike, and the drill instructor had completely destroyed our bay. There were clothes and things everywhere. That night, we had to mix soap, sand, and water and get down on our hands and knees and scrub the floor.

Friday. They issued us long underwear due to the nippy weather. Friday night I took over my first billet as company gunnery sergeant. I guess I did all right. I haven't gotten my evaluation yet. Almost everyone gets an unsatisfactory, so that is probably what I will get. The drill instructor on duty cornered me twice and really reamed me. I guess he just felt it his duty because I wasn't doing anything wrong. At least I don't think I was.

Today, Saturday, we had a weapons and personnel inspection. I really lucked out. First of all, it rained, so we didn't have to go outside. Secondly, Lieutenant Long, our cadre platoon commander, didn't look too closely at my stuff or ask me anything I couldn't answer. Consequently, I came through without any wear and tear. If it had been Sergeant Howard, our drill instructor, it would have been all over! He misses nothing.

Monday. We have a test on the rifle and bayonet. I have to study this weekend.

Our platoon started out with sixty-three officer candidates. It is or will be down to about forty-eight or forty-nine candidates by the end of the week. Most of these just weren't physically able to handle it.

Everyone gets a chit for one thing or another. The yellow one doesn't mean too much. The white one is the killer. Even so, it doesn't count for much unless your drill instructor or platoon commander decides you won't make a good officer.

I will tell you one thing about this place: your appetite is good, and you sleep soundly! I'll bet I am asleep within five minutes of climbing into bed.

Dec. 17, 1968

The other night one of the drill instructors went around and checked for unlocked lockers after we went to bed. And of course, I had forgotten to lock my locker, so I had to get up in the middle of the night, get my rifle, take it to bed, and sleep with it.

Today was pretty easy. We got up at 5:30 a.m. and ran outside for some exercises. Then we ate breakfast and took our test on the M14. We had a critique on the test and some drill. It was too cold out, so we came in early from drill. Lunch, a morals lecture from the chaplain and physical training took up the rest of the day. We are now running two-and-a-half miles a day or more.

Some of the guys in the other bay are singing Christmas carols, and it is really making me homesick! I caught a dandy of a cold. Of course, it is a wonder it has taken this long with everyone coughing on everybody else. All of the colleges around Washington are closed because of the flu, and it is starting to go around here.

Dec. 31, 1968 (after home leave for Christmas)

Sunday night. We moodily nursed our cokes in the canteen, listening to Glen Campbell croon.

"I am a lineman for the county / And I drive the main road / Searchin' in the sun for another overload / And the Wichita lineman is still on the line."

Our Christmas leave was over. We were dreading Monday, starting the whole routine over again.

"I need a small vacation / But it don't look like rain."

Monday reveille would come too soon. There would be a crashing of garbage cans and yelling of the DIs, yanking us from our sleep. A scramble down to the cold pavement for wakeup exercises, then back to shave, make our beds, dress for the day, and out for morning formation. We would hardly have time to take a breath.

Jan. 5, 1969

This week has turned into a real hassle. We went on a seven-mile hike yesterday, and it was a killer. We ran almost the whole way, up and down hills. There were only about ten or twelve of us who didn't get straggling chits. Then we came back and had to take everything out of our squad bay and clean it for the hundredth time. I only got a chance to read one letter from home last night and that was under the blanket with a flashlight after lights out. I barely had time to take a shower. The night before, I didn't have time for even that!

The next two or three weeks are going to be a real hassle. We will be on the go constantly. But after that, it should get better. Right now, I am in a history review class. After this, we have two hours of physical training. I am really sore from the last hike.

We ran three miles yesterday and three and a half the day before. Not too many made the three-and-a-half miler. I did though. We ran wind sprints before the run plus regular physical training. Wow, they have really been putting the pressure on around here. Next week is going to be a tough one and so is the week after, but every week is a step closer to graduation.

I had better close now and start studying for our history test Monday. Platoon Commander, Lieutenant Long, gave my bunkmate and me a little lecture on our low grades. He said we never straggle, had pretty-high peer evaluations, and not-bad leadership grades, but we needed the knowledge, so we better hop to it and study. Of course, my bunkmate, Denny, has higher grades on everything else. So he got a longer lecture. Most of my grades, except academic, are higher than average. Consequently, I guess Lt. Long felt I rated a lecture too. All of my academic grades are passing, but they are low passing. My academic average is seventy-five for three tests. Seventy is passing.

Part of the evaluation process includes peer evaluations. Peer evaluations are important and stressful. Each of us has to rank everyone else in the platoon from the best, number one, to the worst, number sixty-three, if that is the number of candidates in the platoon. They play a significant role in who stays and who doesn't.

Jan. 12, 1969

This has really been a busy week. We had an overnight compass course Monday. Naturally, it snowed Monday night, and we froze. The march to the compass course was unbelievable. I call it march facetiously because we had to run the whole way to keep up. Only twelve of us in my platoon and seven in another platoon made it! The drill instructors got us up at 4:30 Tuesday morning to march home.

Tuesday. We had the confidence course. That wasn't too bad. Wednesday, we had the speed march reaction course. That involved running about three-and-a-half miles, over hills, and then solving a problem at the end. This is all done after running the obstacle course.

Today, we were issued clothing in the morning, practiced marching, and had physical training in the afternoon. It was a killer. I was hurting and so was everyone else. We spent all evening cleaning the barracks. I am really tired. Tonight from 1 a.m. to 3 a.m., I have to get up and stand guard in the parking lot. Then tomorrow, we have either a seven- or nine-mile hike, mostly a run. I have a few minutes, so I think I will take a quick shower.

Friday morning. Right now, I am sitting in a first aid class, waiting for it to begin. They are supposed to show a really gory movie. I don't think I will watch.

That movie was gross! It showed doctors fixing up a man who had both legs blown off, was blind, and his face burned black. Ugh! The movie actually pictured the surgeons amputating his legs, peeling off his skin, and removing his eyes. The guy next to me fainted and fell out of his chair. Another guy keeled over while standing in formation outside. The movie was graphic and gory but ended by noting that the subject married his nurse. I guess that tidbit was to provide a little bit of hope to an otherwise truly gloomy scenario.

Either tonight or tomorrow, I will be candidate platoon sergeant. It is a very hot place to be because sometimes they really dump on you. I hope I get by okay.

Saturday. I was candidate platoon sergeant, and I survived! I am a nervous wreck but still alive. My bunkmate's knee has gotten pretty bad. I am not sure he will be able to finish the program. I sure hope he can. He is a great guy. Since we have started, we have lost twenty-three people.

Wow, quite a few! Before we are through, we will probably lose five or six more.

The duty drill instructor caught a guy in my platoon smoking. He had to put a trash can over his head and smoke a whole pack of cigarettes, three at a time. By the time he finished, he was throwing up all over everything.

I didn't go to Washington. My bunkmate, Denny, couldn't leave because he is hurt, and I didn't want to go without him. Well, I am pretty tired, as usual, so I think I will go to bed.

Jan. 16, 1969

We lost another candidate. We were standing in front of our bunks about 5:30 a.m., waiting for morning physical training. This guy just keeled over and passed out. They wheeled him away in an ambulance, unconscious. That was the last we saw of him.

It is Wednesday of the seventh week. Another week, and the tough part will be over. I can hardly wait. I am having a hard time keeping the proper attitude toward the physical part of this program. Even though things have been easier physically lately, I have to make myself keep going. Maybe they have just worn my body down, or maybe I am just tired of it, or both. Besides, I am pretty sure of making it. I got a satisfactory chit for platoon sergeant, my first, which is really a big deal.

The discipline around here isn't letting up any. The word is that we are an experimental group, and they are hitting discipline pretty hard. Supposedly, the other platoons stress teamwork, but our platoon stresses individual performance.

I am tired constantly. We have had a little time the last two nights. I hope it keeps up. Last night for punishment, we did four hundred jumping jacks, one hundred squat thrusts, one hundred leg lifts, and twenty-five push-ups. This is plus regular physical training where we run three miles or better and do a bunch of other exercises.

Jan. 17, 1969

I am sitting here in the squad bay while the rest of the troops are out on a hike. I kind of finked out. I have an infected toe that has been bothering me for the last few weeks. Yesterday, I could hardly walk. We had two short hikes, so I went to sick bay today. I was relieved to get out of the hike. However, Sergeant Howard, our cadre platoon sergeant, threw a guilt trip on me by telling me how disappointed in me he was for missing the hike, staying back with the other malingerers. My words, not his.

Coming from him, it meant something. We all think Staff Sergeant Howard and Lieutenant Long are great role models. Staff Sergeant Howard has a wicked and subtle sense of humor. Laughing or making any noise during an inspection invites personal disaster. However, it is very difficult to keep a straight face listening to the comments Staff Sergeant Howard directs to the various individuals he is inspecting. The exception, of course, would be when he directs his comments to you. That is to be avoided at all costs!

On one occasion, we were all standing at attention, waiting to be inspected. Our equipment was laid out behind us on our bunks. Staff Sergeant Howard slowly proceeded down the row of bunks, examining our equipment and each of us. I held my breath as he passed by me. Two bunks down something caught his eye. He stopped abruptly, squared up on candidate Jones (not his name), grabbed the candidate's rifle, turned it up, looked down the barrel, whipped it back to check the action, and upside down to look at the butt plate. All the while, he continued to comment about the increasing amount of sand he was seeing. The amount of sand grew with each new exclamation. By the time Staff Sergeant Howard was finished with candidate Jones, you would swear that candidate Jones had brought the beach in with him and was standing waist deep in sand. It was very funny but to utter a sound would be to invite a personal catastrophe. Ultimately, candidate Jones got caught smoking on fire watch. He was shipped off to Parris Island the following day to train as an enlisted Marine.

Another time, Staff Sergeant Howard was holding a class on protocol. One candidate, brave soul that he was, asked a question. Staff Sergeant Howard responded, "What are you asking me, candidate? Are you trying to bait me, candidate?" Staff Sergeant Howard's voice elevated, "Are you?" The candidate was doing his best to deny the whole situation, wishing, no doubt, he had never asked the question. Staff Sergeant Howard continued more calmly, "You know, candidate, if you continue to bait me, you will become a master baiter. Is that what you want, candidate, to be known as the masturbator?" Despite a lot of faces red with suppressed laughter among the rest of us, not a sound was heard.

Lt. Long stayed cool and aloof. He knew how to wear the uniform. When we finally achieved a status where we could put on our greens, he provided all the tips on how to make the uniform look just right on us. We wanted our uniforms to look as good on us as his did on him. He also attempted to pass along some of his wisdom gained in Vietnam. In one instance, he talked about his platoon taking fire and how, rather than reacting immediately, he would take a minute to review his options. He considered what he had done the last time he took fire before deciding on a course of action. Never having been in that situation, we were all ears.

It seems to me quite a few guys could be kicked out the tenth week. That would sure be crummy. They told Denny Cox, my bunkmate, they would graduate him no matter what if he could get the doctor's okay on his knee. He was a great officer candidate. As it turned out, though, his knee didn't hold up, and he was discharged.

Jan. 20, 1969

Right now, we are giving our impromptu speeches. I just gave mine on "While we are sleeping, could our National Guard really defend us?" Having been in one of the

National Guard units sent into the Watts Riots, I had serious doubts, but I guess I did okay on the speech. Yesterday, we had squad tactics. It was miserable. It rained all day. We were soaked, and the hikes there and back were bears. Plus I messed up my squad tactics problem. Everything went okay except I got lost. The lieutenant who was in charge of the problem got so red in the face, I thought he was about to have a heart attack.

Jan. 21, 1969

Tuesday. I am back in class, listening to impromptus again. The hard rain keeps us from going outside, so we are giving speeches. I am having a heck of a time keeping my eyes open. We have one more fairly hard week after this. Next Monday, on my birthday, we have the twenty-four-hour war. A helicopter will drop us off in the countryside. We play war all day and night. It will be cold!

Friday. The last hard day. We have a nine-mile hike today. Not too bad except it is really muddy out and that makes it rough. Monday. We have the twenty-four-hour war. That will be cold and uncomfortable but not too strenuous. Besides, it is downhill after that.

Jan. 30, 1969

We finished our twenty-four-hour war. It got down to seven degrees. I was never so cold in my life. On top of that, in my opinion, the whole thing was a big waste of time. I spent most of my time, virtually all night, lying on cold hard ground shivering. If I don't come down with pneumonia this week, I never will.

They have quit giving chits and posting billets. They also called about six guys in and told them they were going to the board that makes decisions on candidates staying or leaving the program. I guess that means I've made it, and all I am waiting for is the Feb. 7th graduation. Twenty-eight guys have been dropped, and six more, right now, are questionable. They really have weeded this platoon down.

I graduate Friday, and we have guard Thursday.

Feb. 7, 1969

Graduation was great! My father and Red, my wife, attended. Dad pinned on my bars. We all lined up to be saluted by Staff Sergeant Howard, our platoon sergeant. We shook hands with him and palmed him a silver dollar. The salute and silver dollar are a time-honored Marine Corps ritual. He was a great role model who commanded our respect. Carried away by emotion, I told him that if I went into combat, I wanted him there. He probably was thinking he was glad he wouldn't be there. I don't think he had any illusions about his officer candidates, now brand-new second lieutenants.

The Basic School

We operated night and day, trying to cram in all the knowledge we would need to lead a platoon of young Marines in Vietnam. While officer candidate school was a screening process for Marine Corps officers, The Basic School was where new lieutenants learned the nuts and bolts of being a Marine Corps officer.

The Marine Corps takes great pride in every Marine being first and foremost an infantryman. Every Marine Corps officer attends The Basic School. All officers and enlisted Marines when they are in boot camp are trained in basic infantry tactics even though they may specialize in something else.

For me, The Basic School was a great, invigorating experience with something new and exciting virtually every day and/or night. We learned everything from movement to contact and tactics to the use of supporting arms and map reading. A strong emphasis on leadership pervaded every skill taught. It was five months of exciting, intense, and highly satisfying work. I met other young officers with whom I still feel a strong comradeship.

The Basic School culminated in our assignment to a particular branch of arms in the Marine Corps. I chose, and was assigned, to the infantry. That was a pretty safe bet since almost everyone was assigned to the infantry. The exceptions would be those who ranked high in the class and chose other specialties such as armor, artillery, supply, transport, or air traffic control.

2

After a thirty-day leave, I attended recon replacement school at Camp Pendleton, California. The school lasted a few weeks and consisted mostly of refining our ability to call in supporting arms (i.e., artillery, air strikes, and Naval gunfire). It was a nice interlude that allowed me to spend time with my family before going to Vietnam.

Commissioned 2nd Lieutenant with my dad and Red

4

The 7th Marine Regiment

The briefing officer erased the numbers on the large map and wrote six KIA (killed in action), adding fifteen WIA (wounded in action). An enlisted Marine came in with more information. The briefer again erased his numbers replacing them with eight KIA and seventeen WIA.

The officers with me must have been thinking, "Man, you are really in for it." I had just been assigned to the 7^{Th} Marine Regiment, the unit taking the casualties recorded on the briefer's map. The other officers were assigned to other units: Graff to the 1st Marines, Erins to the 5th Marines, and Hodgins to the 26th Marines. We were in the 1st Marine Division headquarters, receiving our intelligence briefing prior to being sent to our units. Despite the numbers, I was more excited than scared—no doubt a reflection of my naivety. I had yet to work out that none of us were immune from being recorded as one of those casualty figures inscribed on the briefer's map.

In August 1969, I left for Vietnam, one of six from my basic school company to go directly to Vietnam. My parents and my wife, Red, saw me off at the airport. I will say that until I later saw my son, Lt. Adam Curry, an infantry officer with the 82nd Airborne Division, off to Iraq, I had no appreciation for how they must have felt. I was superstitious enough not to want anyone to wish me good luck or any of that stuff. No melodrama. Just goodbye. I'll see you in a year.

August 19, 1969

We landed at Clark Air Force Base in the Philippines. A typhoon prevented us from going directly to Okinawa. Clark Air Force Base is a well-kept base with lots of mowed lawns and a busy officers' club. The bachelor officers quarters on base was full, so we were billeted off base at a hotel.

The most notable thing about the trip to our hotel was the machine gun post in the middle of the town square. Apparently, it was there to deter any action from the Philippines' long running insurgency. At some point well before we got there, the heads of two guards from Clark Air force Base had been found in a dumpster.

August 20, 1969

I am in a hot little hotel room near Clark Air Force Base. My feet are raw and sore from my shoes, and my uniform is filthy. I should have brought some civilian clothes along, but who can foresee a typhoon? I spotted my uncle,

Mike Patterson, an Air Force pilot I had last seen in Virginia where he is stationed. He was walking across the road while I was in a jeep on the way to the hotel. What a coincidence! I got the driver to stop while I hopped out to say hello. Unfortunately, I only talked to him a little because I was dead tired. My hard-core basic school buddies in the jeep gave me a hard time because I did not salute him, he being a major, and I a lowly second lieutenant.

I left Sunday and arrived here Wednesday. I missed Tuesday altogether, or maybe I missed Monday, one of the two. I felt crummy the whole trip, the usual headache. I got to my humble hotel room in The Oasis, took a shower, and had to drip dry. There were no towels.

August 21, 1969

We had to stay here another day, so we rented a car and went to Manila, a really interesting city! Whenever we stopped, a chattering group of kids surrounded us, asking for handouts. I didn't know how to respond. Mike Hodgins, from my basic school company, threw the kids a handful of American coins. That created a mad scramble. The Philippine peso is worth about twenty-five cents.

Our visit to the main market, if nothing else, was instructional, having never been exposed to anything like it. It was a cacophony of sounds and a malodorous symphony of smells, for which I had no appreciation. It got to the point where I had to hold my nose and breathe through my mouth.

The Philippines was beautiful, filled with vibrant colors and an array of brilliant green foliage. I am glad I live in America though. The poverty was obvious. They don't even use outhouses. I guess they just use the bushes or fields. In the Philippines, armed guards appeared everywhere. That didn't make one feel very secure, considering the war was supposed to be in Vietnam.

August 22, 1969

At last, I am here in Okinawa at Camp Hanson. What a hole! Clark AFB was a paradise, a big country club. The Air Force certainly doesn't rough it. It looks as if I won't be going to the 3rd Marine Division, maybe the 1st Marine Division. I find out later today. Apparently, we will sit around here for a couple of days. I hope not too long because it is such a hole.

August 24, 1969

I have been reassigned from the 3rd Marine Division to the 1st Marine Division, and I leave Okinawa the twenty-seventh. I don't know if I can stand three more days of this place. There is absolutely nothing to do but hang around the officers club and drink. Our rooms are real sweatboxes, and the water is turned off half the time. We have to muster twice a day, so we can't go anywhere, as if there is anywhere to go.

We store all of the uniforms and luggage we brought in Okinawa. I have no idea why we were told to bring all of our uniforms. They will just sit in storage. We also get the remainder of our shots here. Some of those really hurt! The gamma globulin shot can make even a battle-hardened gunnery sergeant tear up. There was much wailing and gnashing of teeth in the line while waiting to get our shots. A number of us were sitting very gingerly the next day.

Of the five of us that came together, John Erins and Mike Hodgins leave tonight for Da Nang. Jim House, John Graff, and I follow on the twenty-seventh unless we are moved up on the list.

August 25, 1969

I am slowly going stir crazy. There is absolutely nothing to do but hang around the Officers' Club. At least there they have the air-conditioning working. Sleep is hard to come by because our rooms are so hot!

August 27, 1969

Arriving in Vietnam I was little nervous. I halfway expected to get off of the plane in the middle of an attack with mortar shells bursting around me. We had flown in a commercial aircraft with civilian stewardesses and arrived at a big busy airport, operating with business as usual. Much to my disappointment, I wasn't handed a helmet and flak jacket and pointed to the nearest bunker but directed to the area where I was supposed to report with my orders for transportation to my unit. It was all very businesslike, not the least dramatic. There was even a barracks for those who had to wait overnight.

One thing that literally hit me with a wallop when I got off the plane was the heat! It was like being enveloped by a suffocating blanket. The heat drained the energy and sucked the breath right out of me. My uniform instantly became a perspiration sodden mess. There was no way to be adequately prepared for Vietnam's heat.

August 29, 1969

Right now, I am at the 1st Marine Division headquarters, awaiting transportation to the 7th Marine Regiment. The 1st Marine Division headquarters is built on a hillside ringed on three sides by mountains and on the fourth side by Da Nang and the sea. It is impossible to hit with mortars or rockets.

There is nothing private about going to the head (toilet) here. I was coming out of the shower with my towel just as all the Vietnamese women came to work. That wasn't too bad. After all, I had my towel. However, I downright resent tipping my hat to them while sitting on the head. The toilets are a series of seats built over cut-off barrels in a wooden enclosure screened in front by wire mesh and situated next to a path. Using them can turn into a social occasion, particularly if people parade by while you or whoever else is sitting there. It was very awkward, to say the least, to be occupying the head as the officers club workers filed by at their shift change. They must have become used to it because it didn't seem to faze them.

August 30, 1969

I am still at the 1st Marine Division headquarters. What a mess! I wonder how the Marine Corps ever win any wars. Yesterday evening, they gave my orders to a lieutenant going to amtracs. I spent all day today waiting for my orders to be sent back. Personnel called amtracs several times, and they were told each time that my orders were about to leave. Well, it is now 4 p.m., and I am still waiting. I have been doing a slow burn. The unit I am going to has been in contact the last two or three days, and I would like to get down there before everyone packs up and goes home. Famous last words!

Everyone around here has a flak jacket and helmet but me. That makes me feel very insecure. They also have pistols. However, a pistol wouldn't do me any good anyway because the best I could hope for with a pistol is to scare someone with the noise.

September 3, 1969

I got to the 7th Marine Regiment at landing zone (LZ) Baldy and received the runaround for a couple of days. The division likes to give new people a week to acclimatize (no way) so that the new guy won't get killed the first week. At any rate, I didn't know if I was coming or going. The ending was spectacular though! I was rushed over to my battalion at LZ Ross the minute it came in from the field, given my gear and my platoon, and left that night on an operation. Wow! What a rush.

The company came in to Fire Base Ross for a hot meal. After the meal, they immediately left the base to begin another operation. As the company lined up to receive their meals, one Marine had an accidental discharge (all rifles were supposed to have been cleared upon entering the base). That created quite a stir! It would have been a heck of a note to get shot while getting my meal before even going to the field!

When I picked up my platoon, it was a dark, rainy night. I was introduced to my platoon sergeant and, of course, promptly forgot his name. The platoon sergeant introduced me to my squad leaders and the platoon guide. Naturally, I immediately forgot their names too. In the dark, they all looked alike. Fortunately, I soon met my radioman called Bo. That name I could remember, and with him having the radio, I could always recognize him.

We marched most of the night to our starting point and collapsed toward morning alongside the road. Though drenched clear through, we wrapped ourselves in our poncho and poncho liner, lay down in the mud, and slipped into an exhausted sleep. We dug no holes, posted no sentries, nothing. We all could have had our throats cut and would never have known the difference.

The next morning, we started a sweep. I was loaded down with equipment: helmet, flak jacket, pack, M16, web gear, canteens, ammo pouches, first-aid pouch, grenades, the works. The gear I was issued at battalion was very worn. I would swear my flak jacket had bloodstains from its previous owner, though that may have been my imagination. The suspenders holding up my pistol belt definitely were of WWII vintage as was my backpack. I might add that there weren't enough compasses for everyone, so the only guy in the platoon with a compass was a squad leader. Fortunately, I brought my own jungle boots because jungle boots were not part of the issue either.

I was covered in every piece of armor I could wear. Being new and having heard all the gory stories, my main fear was that I would trigger a booby trap. In wet terrain and unbearable heat, we walked up and over paddy dikes through tree lines and hedgerows. We changed direction several times as someone higher up changed the plan. By afternoon, with all the weight of my equipment and the heat and humidity, I was staggering along just trying to keep up. I definitely was not acclimatized!

We finally stopped. I immediately dumped all of my gear, rifle, helmet, and flak jacket included. Our commanding officer (CO), Captain Stanat, called for the platoon commanders. We were deployed in a line across a series of rice paddies. Captain Stanat was holding his conference on a raised mound, probably an old grave. He was near the front of the column, and I was at the back with the Third Platoon, my platoon.

My platoon sergeant and I made our way to Captain Stanat's position. We no sooner arrived than the enemy opened up on us with automatic weapons. Everyone was hugging the ground. My platoon sergeant was shaking (it was near the end of his second tour), and my adrenalin was soaring. Lying prone on the ground, Captain Stanat turned to me. "Lieutenant, take Third Platoon and envelop that tree line." He indicated the area from which we were taking fire. That meant crawling back across all the paddies separating me from my platoon with bullets flying. No helmet, flak jacket, or rifle.

Passing a wounded Marine receiving aid from the corpsman, I crawled back, scrunching up and lunging head and shoulders, then rear end over the paddy dikes in a caterpillar-like movement. I was operating under the theory that if I got shot, it would be in the rear end since that was the last part over the dike.

I got back to my platoon and yelled, "Guns up!" I set up a base of fire and swept the area with my machine guns. The shooting stopped, but I was reluctant to have my platoon get on line and walk across the open rice paddy. If the enemy were still there, we would take far too many casualties. I looked to my platoon sergeant, tapping his experience. He said, "Lieutenant, why don't you send a couple of scouts across before sending the platoon." I did. Two Marines got up and cautiously walked across the open ground. The enemy was gone. We swept the area but found nothing.

Watching those two Marines get up and walk across those wide-open rice paddies, it really hit me how important it was to make good decisions. A decision I made could literally mean life or death. It was an awesome responsibility for anyone, much less a young, inexperienced second lieutenant. The fact that those two Marines would get up and walk across an open field demonstrates the discipline instilled by the Marine Corps as well as the courage of those young Marines.

After sweeping the paddies, we moved up into the mountains for the night. I set up in my platoon headquarters and began to clean my rifle. Unfortunately, we had been trained with the M14 rifle, and I had to suffer the indignity of having the corpsman show me how to break down my M16 so I could clean it. I was glad none of my Marine Corps buddies were there to see the Navy showing me how to clean my rifle. I would never have lived it down! That night, I slept right next to my hole with my rifle in one hand and helmet in the other. If you want to call it sleep.

September 5, 1969

I led my first platoon patrol. We were sent to explore the surrounding foothills for trails. After a short walk, we came to a trail that branched off in three directions. I set up a patrol base with my platoon sergeant and radio operator and sent a squad up each branch. Within a few minutes, bursts of automatic fire broke out down one of the trail branches. We all hit the deck. The squad leader radioed, "One confirmed enemy KIA (killed in action) and one enemy WIA (wounded in action)." There was a moment of silence, then a single gunshot. The squad leader radioed back, "We now have two enemy KIAs."

When the squad leader got back, we got all the gory details, including brains being splattered. I sort of lost interest in the meatballs and beans I was eating at the time. Everybody seemed to think that it was pretty good, two kills for the new lieutenant, but I couldn't see how I had much to do with it.

September 8, 1969

After two days and about five changes in plans, we continued to move into the mountains. At times, we had to hack our way through the undergrowth. It wasn't really jungle, more like high, thick bushes. Captain Stanat became very agitated over our slow progress and ordered me to get up to the front of my platoon, as we were the lead platoon, and bust my way through. Since the longevity of the people up front is not great, in The Basic School, we were taught to stay right behind the lead squad. I wasn't overly eager to be up there. But my CO was right behind me, so I didn't have much choice. I positioned myself right behind the point as he, using a machete, broke brush, forcing his way through the heavy growth. I rotated the point as each became exhausted with the exertion. We were all bathed in sweat. Finally, we found a trail leading to the top of the mountain, our objective.

My platoon had been on the trail awhile when I stopped them so I could find our position on the map. By this time, I was in my usual position behind the point squad, and the CO had gone elsewhere. It occurred to me that I ought to put out security while we were stopped. I was just telling the platoon sergeant to do it when bullets started flying. Everyone hit the deck. I thought my goose was cooked since we were sitting in a line on the trail. We had been told hair-raising stories in The Basic School of entire units being wiped out in ambushes.

I immediately began yelling for the machine guns, "Guns up!" "Get the grenade launcher working!" "Squads on line!" We put out a lot of suppressing firepower. Fortunately, the enemy, there were only three as it turned out, showed their poor marksmanship, or at the least were as startled as we were.

The only casualty we took was a man with a small fragment in his heel. That probably was caused by one of our own M79 rounds exploding prematurely. We were lucky. The point man had seen the three enemy soldiers walking toward him on the trail. He tried to shoot them but had forgotten to chamber a round. By the time he did, the enemy saw him, and everyone started shooting.

We could tell from a heavy blood trail that one of the enemy was badly wounded. We followed his blood trail for a short distance and then were ordered to wait for one of the other platoons to catch up with us. They had taken four prisoners that day, one a lieutenant colonel as we later found out. We spent the night there on a plateau we had used as a landing zone to get out the prisoners, my casualty, and some sick Marines.

Several small plateaus were stair-stepped up the mountainside, probably abandoned fields. Our trail ran along one side of the plateaus, and a stream bordered the other side. Foliage and large rocks surrounded the trail and plateaus. The platoon sergeant took me aside. "Lieutenant, tone down the yelling. It is a good way to get shot. With all that noise, you draw attention to yourself." I took his advice to heart.

The next day, the CO had my platoon come to his position, which was near a stream. We were to clean up before going out on a patrol. I set my platoon in a perimeter on a plateau below the captain's and went up to see him. I no sooner got to his position, then he said, "Lieutenant Curry, what's the deal on the prisoner?"

"What prisoner, sir?" I had no idea what he was talking about. Apparently, while I was on my way to see the CO, some Marines had walked over to the stream and caught an enemy soldier standing in the stream right in front of our perimeter.

On the trail between our perimeter and the stream lay the body of a dead enemy soldier. Whenever we went to wash or fill our canteens, we would gingerly step over him. This was the first dead person I had really seen up close and personal. I wasn't quite sure how to handle the situation. On the one hand, I wanted to look like a veteran. On the other hand, I didn't want to look at him and get sick. That would have been a little hard to explain. One thing about which there was no doubt, I didn't breath through my nose at any time while in his vicinity! As it turned out, he looked just like a wax dummy, so it was no big thing, at least until he started to swell, and his skin began to peel. One of the troops remarked that he couldn't help but think of the dead soldier every time a fly landed in his food. After that, I couldn't either.

After my platoon had washed and eaten, we were sent out on a patrol. Within a short walk, we came upon an empty enemy base camp, actually two camps. In the first, the largest, we found all sorts of gear. The base camp was tucked into a formation of rocks. A sleeping platform in the middle had an earthen oven off to one side. The rocks formed all sorts of little caves and nooks and crannies. Hidden in these places we found a ton of rice, mortars, machine guns, rocket-propelled grenades (RPG), and a lot of other gear. The more stuff we found, the more nervous I got. I figured the enemy wouldn't leave something behind as important to them as mortars.

I took my first serious casualty here. Three Marines were together, looking for more equipment. One of them got in front of the other two without them knowing it. He popped up in front of the two Marines, and one of them, mistaking him for the enemy, shot him. He was hit in the side. We stopped the bleeding and medevaced him immediately. He was conscious and talking. Hopefully, he will be all right.

A little later in the day, I did a very stupid thing. I sent two of my squad leaders along with two other men to check out the area and look for ambush sites. The stupid part was sending the squad leaders where they both could be hit at the same time.

A short time after the fire team left, the enemy opened up on us. The bullets were going high, but I was ducking anyway. I could hear them cracking overhead. At about the same time, my fire team ran into trouble. I got a frantic radio call saying they were pinned down by many NVA and that all four Marines were wounded. I quickly got my platoon together and started off in the direction of the shooting. I was expecting to get shot every time I crossed a little open ground.

We didn't end up finding any enemy. Only one Marine was seriously wounded, the same man who had shot his friend earlier in the day. He was hit just above the groin. As he observed while we were carrying him to the LZ, he'd had a very bad day.

We stayed in the base camp for a couple of days along with the CP group and another platoon. It rained. Everyone was sick including me. The place stank of rotting rice, human feces, vomit, stagnant water, and garbage. On top of that, it didn't seem to me a very good defensive position. I was expecting the NVA to try to take their mortars back.

Throughout the night, I could hear explosions as someone on watch would hear a noise, get nervous, and throw a grenade. One of those nights, I could not have cared less. I was so sick, I literally couldn't move. I lay on the muddy ground in the rain, in the middle of the base camp, wracked with spasms of vomiting and diarrhea. I was filthy. Fortunately by morning, I felt okay. I made use of the small stream running through the base camp to thoroughly scrub my clothes and myself.

The CO finally told me to take my platoon back to the stream where we had bathed a few days before. By this time, the dead enemy soldier who had been on the trail near the stream was quite ripe. I thought it prudent to send a squad ahead to bury him. The selected squad really sent up some moaning and wailing when I told them. It was the ultimate blow to their ego to have to bury an enemy soldier. One they hadn't even killed, at that. It took some time afterward for them to regain their composure. One sniff, and anyone within two hundred yards could tell that he did need burying.

We stayed by the stream that night. The next morning, the rest of the company moved out of the base camp and blew it up. Later, Captain Stanat told me to send someone back to the base camp to make sure it had been destroyed. I sent a fire team. They walked right up on three NVA looking through the camp. The fire team killed two of them and wounded another who later died while waiting to be medevaced.

That evening we started an arduous all night march back to LZ Baldy for a 24-hour rest period. It was very confusing. Part of the time the company was lost. My platoon, in the rear of the column, constantly scrambling to keep up with the rest as the column expanded and contracted. I was worried we would lose someone in the pitch-black night. While the other platoons stopped for rest breaks, my platoon spent the time closing up and counting off to make sure everyone was accounted for. Rumor had it that on a previous all-night march, a Marine who had fallen asleep during a rest stop had been left. His mutilated body was found the next day. It wasn't just a rumor, it happened. It was a corpsman, I think. I wanted to make sure that didn't happen to one of us. By the time we arrived at LZ Baldy, I was exhausted. I would have much preferred to remain in the mountains.

September 11, 1969

After a twenty-four-hour rest period, we were alerted for another mission. This involved being lifted by helicopter from LZ Ross into an area where we were to set up a blocking force. Another unit was detailed to sweep the enemy toward us.

We moved by truck from LZ Baldy to LZ Ross, which was smaller than LZ Baldy. The Marines had occupied it after the Army left. The 7th Marines patrolled aggressively around LZ Ross, which resulted in numerous enemy contacts. Actually, those were the casualties I saw posted on the board at 1st Marines Division headquarters when I arrived in the country.

I was in the back of a truck with other members of my platoon in a convoy, speeding toward LZ Ross. Horn blowing, we were flying down a narrow road lined with foot traffic, bicycles, motorbikes, and vehicles going in the other direction. I don't know how we avoided hitting one of them.

A truck somewhere ahead hit a mine. I could see pillars of smoke and flames from the crippled vehicles. Medevac choppers (helicopters) with casualties were zinging by us heading for First Med (hospital). As we passed the burned-out trucks, I sat anxiously expecting another mine to blow at any time. The anxiety added to the general discomfort of riding in the back of the truck and wondering which part of my anatomy would be most impacted by an explosion coming through the bed of the truck. I removed my flak jacket and sat on it.

The air assault was a new experience. It all seemed to happen in a rush. There was no opportunity to plan. As the birds (helicopters) came in, I was trying to divide the leadership of my platoon into different groups. That was what we were taught to do at The Basic School. The whole leadership wouldn't all be killed at once if a bird crashed. Captain Stanat was in too much of a hurry for that to be relevant. He shoved us all onto the same bird. Luckily, it was not a contested landing. I got my platoon out of the helicopter and set up a perimeter. We were the first platoon into the LZ; hence, my concern with dividing the leadership. As the rest of the company landed, we consolidated the perimeter and then moved to our assigned areas.

September 13, 1969

So far, this week has been easy. My platoon is set up around the company CP. We run a patrol in the morning and a squad ambush at night. A little river flows near us.

Everyone strips and lies in it during the heat of the day. It is hot! Good thing we have the stream because the area is mostly sandy soil and low scrub brush. There are no shade trees, and the ponchos the men have rigged up to provide some shade trap the heat. Sitting under the poncho feels like being in an oven.

The Vietnamese countryside is beautiful. Rice paddies with the occasional water buffalo set against a verdant background. It certainly belies the violence. So far, the regiment has been keeping us clear away from any civilization. We are a couple of miles southeast of the Song Thu Bon River.

The Marines over here, mainly nineteen- to twenty-year-olds, are amazing, smart, brave, and extremely mature. I don't believe the critics of our youth could ever have seen these young men. I don't think our college hippy or frat rats can compare. They are all children in comparison. War will quickly turn a boy into a man.

Presweetened Kool-Aid and candy are hot items from home. The Kool-Aid flavors our canteen water. Between the taste of the plastic canteen and the purifying Halazone tablets, the water tastes terrible. It needs a little flavor.

It seems to me that this war is a big waste. People are being killed, and nothing is being accomplished. I suppose that can be said for a lot in life. No one can say this is a civilized world because people are fighting each other all over it and for the damnedest reasons.

Boy, I became a veteran fast. I got shot at the first day, jungle rot the second day, and the runs on the third day. What a record!

September 14, 1969

I just got back from my first-night ambush. It was a can of worms! The first thing that went wrong was when I tried to register firing points for the artillery. The mortar squad said we were one place on the map, and I said we were another. I tried to call a fire mission using mills, as we were taught. The mortar squad had no idea what I was talking about. Consequently, when they fired for us to register a target, we couldn't see where the rounds were landing. Not knowing where a round would land made me increasingly reluctant to call for more rounds. As it continued to get darker, I told the mortars they were close enough and let it go at that.

Next, I waited till it got too dark to move into the ambush site. We went right past it and had to turn around and backtrack. By then, it was really dark, so everyone jumped into the weeds, not knowing where everyone else was. I wasn't going to get up and go wandering around in the dark to find out.

To top it off, we ended up on the wrong side of about a thirty-degree slope. We spent the whole night slipping down and crawling back up again. I don't know how that happened because we were supposed to be lying above the trail instead of below it.

The mosquitoes provided the finishing touch. I swear they rode horses and traveled in herds. They were unrelentingly vicious.

From the noise level, I thought I was in the Los Angeles Airport. Marines snored on my left and right. The guy next to me rattled the bushes all night, swatting mosquitoes and cussing. Every three minutes someone on the radio asked, "Mike three, are you secure?" which I am sure could be heard for miles. I felt like telling him we would be more secure if he would just shut up. Then, of course, the rains came amidst a chorus of curses from everyone.

The ambush was back from the trail and in the weeds far enough so that had the enemy come, we would have never known it. The enemy had to have been deaf, dumb, blind, and half dead not to know we were there. It wasn't one of my finer operations!

September 16, 1969

We set up an ambush last night that was perfect in all respects, except no one walked into it, and I got hurt moving into the ambush site.

That afternoon, I got with a departing Marine and swapped my WWII Marine Corps issue pack for a rucksack, the kind carried by the Army and South Vietnamese soldiers. The advantage of the rucksack was it could hold more gear than the small one I had, a two-edged sword because more gear meant more weight. When we moved out to our ambush site, I was wearing all of my gear: helmet, flak jacket, cartridge belt, four canteens, rifle, ammunition, and my pack.

The ambush site was on elevated ground alongside a trail. We found some food containers that led us to believe the enemy was using the trail. I set everybody into position, climbing, directing, and harassing. As I moved up on some large rocks to my place in the ambush, my knee gave way. I couldn't straighten it. I had torn a cartilage wrestling before I joined the Marine Corps and that was the knee that collapsed. Throughout the night I kept hoping the knee would straighten itself out, which it had done before. Unfortunately, it didn't, and ultimately, I called it in to the company commander. He sounded very skeptical when I told him.

However, when morning came and the knee still didn't work, he called a medevac helicopter. It was rather humiliating to be carried on a poncho liner to the helicopter. Even worse, one of the Marines carrying me collapsed due to the heat and had to be medevaced as well.

I was flown to LZ Baldy, then to a triage facility in Da Nang. There, they make life-and-death decisions on the priority of treatment of the badly wounded—who can be saved and who cannot. Fortunately, none of it applied to me. I was flown from there to the hospital ship USS Sanctuary.

We landed on the ship's helicopter pad. Corpsmen rushed me on a litter to a receiving room and cut off all of my clothes, including my precious jungle boots. They made a diagnosis and sent me into the bowels of the ship for treatment.

5

Guam

September 17, 1969

On a gurney, I was wheeled into the main treatment room on the ship. I could see seriously hurt people everywhere. The treatment of a Marine with a dislocated shoulder he got falling out of the back of a truck didn't help my raising anxiety.

The doctor looked at him and immediately got on the phone and called another doctor and a couple of corpsmen. I was lying on a gurney waiting my turn for treatment, listening to the conversation.

"Hey, Jack, come and take a look at this!"

"I haven't seen anything like it."

"Have you ever had one like this before?"

"No, I haven't."

"Then we will let you have this one."

The corpsmen, the doctors, and the young Marine all went into a curtained off room. All I could hear were the Marine's pain-filled screams.

"Stop! Stop! It hurts! Stop! Oh my god. You're killing me! *Ah*!"

The doctors came out. One was scratching his head. Over his shoulder, he said to the young Marine, "Next time, we will give you some anesthesia."

All that pain! The screaming! No anesthesia! And the doctors hadn't even gotten his shoulder back in place!

My anxiety peaked! I thoroughly expected the worst. I was lying in a main treatment room in the bowels of the ship, seriously considering various escape options. As it turned out, it wasn't too bad. They shaved my leg, wrapped it up, and put a five-pound weight on the end of it to straighten it, then moved me to a small cubical I shared with a couple another officers.

I just had a great meal with real knives and forks and ice cream! I still haven't gotten a bath, but I figure in a couple of days, they will have to give me a bath in self-defense.

In the ward with me are one guy who rode his jeep over a landmine and another guy who crashed in his helicopter, which leaves a real dilemma in my mind as to the safest way to travel.

The one real difficulty in being in traction is going to the head (bathroom). If I can survive waving to the mama sans while on the head, messing my pants in the field, or trying to find somewhere where no one is sleeping and Charlie (VC) isn't around, then I can get this deal straightened out and down pat.

September 18, 1969

Another zenith reached! Another obstacle trampled beneath my feet! Another Mt. Everest climbed! I held out long enough so I didn't have to use the bedpan! What starry heights will I reach next? My leg has been put in a cast. I got up a couple of times yesterday but hurt too badly and went right back to bed. Today, I got crutches, so I've ventured out into the world of the lounge, just outside the door of my sleeping quarters.

September 19, 1969

Good thing I came in from the field when I did; otherwise, I would have been one mass of jungle rot. It is terrible. I am covered with big ugly pus-covered sores. As it is, I have it on both arms and one leg with my cast on the other leg. At least I look like a veteran. Everyone comes up and says, "What happened, shrapnel?" I just kind of mumble and limp off. Saying, "No, jungle rot," just doesn't sound quite right around all these guys with serious wounds.

September 20, 1969

Right now, I am at the Air Force staging hospital in Da Nang. Tomorrow, I will be on my way to Guam where I will stay for who knows how long. It is a relief to be off the ship because it pitched and rolled so much. I am unsteady on crutches at best, even without the pitch and roll.

They just brought in a Vietnamese woman on a stretcher. She was covered in blood and gore. That is all I know. They just ran by. A plane crashed somewhere, and they expect more patients.

September 21, 1969

I am in Guam. No air-conditioning. What a bummer. We stopped off at the Philippines for about five hours while our plane was refueled and our radar fixed. The whole time we stayed on our litters in the airplane. I think it was a C147 rigged so that stretchers could be put in four tiers like bunk beds. The trip from Da Nang to Clark AFB was perhaps the most pleasant of my life. I was very comfortable, and I spent the journey in a dreamlike state. No doubt the injections we got before we took off had something to do with it.

However, after we took off from Clark, the trip was less pleasant. I was getting restless, plus I had to go to the bathroom. The nurses wouldn't let me get out of my litter to use the plane's facilities, and I was darned if I was going to use a urinal with all those Air Force nurses walking up and down the rows. So I suffered. I got to Guam and the nurses wouldn't give me crutches, so I had to use a urinal anyway with nurses everywhere.

September 22, 1969

This morning, I was taken to the sick officers' quarters. The first thing to greet me was a nurse whose face would stop a stampeding herd of water buffalo, and a smile filled with crooked little yellow teeth. That was a shocker. On top of that, I was put across from a wizened old man who was dying. He was gasping and wheezing and gurgling all the time. I was approached to join a pool on the exact time of his death. That was way too morbid for me.

Our ward is a long open bay with the beds next to each other. A curtain can be pulled to screen the next bed if necessary. Corpsmen, who do most of the work, and nurses walk down the middle of the bay checking patients on either side. There is no privacy.

The guy next to me is named Bill Farwell. I awoke from a nap to watch the bandages on his hand being changed. The doctor had Bill's hand held up. I could see right through it. There was no skin or meat on his hand. It was a startling sight! Eventually, the doctor operated and sewed the hand to a flap of skin on Bill's chest in order to regrow the tissue. He walked around the ward with his hand sewn to his chest.

I have to eat in the ward because the doctor hasn't been to see me. While I am trying to eat in bed, I can lift my eyes off of my plate of food and watch the corpsman shoot liquids down the throat of the toothless, dying, skeletal old man. My appetite hasn't really come around yet.

Down a few beds from me is a major who had his leg blown off. He doesn't utter a word, but I know he is in pain and depressed. Here I am moaning about my aching knee.

I am fast reaching a high state of embarrassment over my jungle rot. Everyone, without fail, looks at my bandages and asks, "How on earth did you get all those wounds?" When I tell them, they seem disappointed, or, in the case of the Red Cross lady, they giggle.

The doctor told me they plan to operate on my knee Thursday, if my jungle rot is cleared up, and I get some movement in my knee. I will have four to six weeks rehab and then back to Vietnam.

September 27, 1969

The old man is still kicking. He moans, groans, mumbles, coughs up sputum, gurgles, and claims he is dying all day and all night. In fact on several occasions, I have been tempted to take my pillow and tippy toe over there and give the good Lord a helping hand. It is fast reaching a point where one of the two of us is going to go: him to the great beyond, or me to the bughouse. From the looks of things, it will be me to the bughouse. The corpsmen say he could get well if he wanted but has made up his mind he is going to die.

September 29, 1969

My jungle rot has finally cleared up, so the doctor will operate Tuesday. Things are humdrum in the hospital, so I thought I would put down a few thoughts on the war in Vietnam.

I think America's reasons and rationale for getting into Vietnam are good. But it is a tragic waste of American lives because the end result, no matter what we do, is a foregone conclusion. The war reminds me of a team of horses hitched to a wagon: one American and one South Vietnamese. The American horse runs like crazy, trying to move the wagon. The other horse just stands there. Consequently, the wagon goes in a big circle.

After six years of war, the two biggest and most vital cities in South Vietnam, Da Nang and Saigon, are not even secure. There is no area in Vietnam we completely control. That is a fact! This is not a purely military war, and we just can't win it by ourselves. The South Vietnamese government appears to be unwilling to put forth the honest effort necessary to win their part of it—the most vital part. Government corruption, apparently, is pervasive. In fact, I think the only real nationalists in the country are the Viet Cong. Too many of the Saigon government are interested in what is in it for them. I am not sorry I came or that I am going back because our government wouldn't be worth a darn if we didn't abide by its decisions. But I resent terribly every American who gets hurt or killed in this country because of the futility of their deaths.

The only people I can find to blame are our military leaders who remain aloof from the dying and the blood. They have misled the president and the public with promises of a sure victory. It is clear there is no such thing, especially the way we are fighting the war. It is even clearer that we can't win when we have to rely on an apathetic South Vietnamese government more interested in making money and living well than in fighting the war. I don't think the Vietnamese farmers, on the whole, care who governs them. The get caught in the middle by both sides. I think they want peace and stability. Right or wrong, my impressions are shared by a great many of the junior officers, the ones who actually fight the war.

November 18, 1969

The doctors have declared me well and fit for duty. My leg isn't working quite like is should. It still is pretty numb and tender. However, it works well enough to be dismissed from the hospital. I will be on my way back to Vietnam via Okinawa. The truth is that I am ready to get back to Vietnam. If I had gone home from the hospital, I think I always would feel like I failed to accomplish what I signed up to do in the first place. I might just as well have stayed in the National Guard and let all the eighteen- and nineteen-year-olds who didn't get in the National Guard continue to fight the war.

6

1st Recon Battalion

December 8, 1969

We were inserted on the observation post (OP) yesterday. Today is rainy and foggy. Fitzsimmons is leading a patrol about two thousand or three thousand meters away from us. He uses us to relay his messages to S3 (operations) at Reconnaissance Battalion. He can't get communications with the battalion. He had several NVA sightings and tried to call in artillery without success. He had a spotter plane overhead for a while, but the fog got too thick, and it had to leave.

Our OP, a small-bunker complex, is on the top of an extremely steep mountain. The bunkers are dug into the ground and reinforced with sandbags. Sandbagged trenches connect the bunkers and sandbagged walls surround the complex. A raised platform in the middle of the complex is used to observe movement in the valley on the trail below. Barbed wire surrounds the complex with a small LZ on a finger of land at one end. Two of the other three sides leading to the OP are precipitous slopes, and the third side is a cliff overlooking the Que Son Valley.

The rats here are huge! I share a bunker with the artillery officer. The bunker has an opening in one wall to a small cave where we store some ordinance. Last night, a rat got caught on something and squeaked and rattled around all night. From the noise he made, I was afraid he would pick up the whole bunker and drag it off with him. When morning came, the artillery officer, armed with a Ka-Bar (Marine fighting knife) and flashlight, went into the ammunition bunker to look for him. I stood by ready to send in reinforcements. Apparently, we not only have to worry about the enemy, we also have to worry about being carried off by rats!

I returned to Vietnam on November 30, 1969, and reported to the personnel office at the 1st Marine Division. I began irritating the personnel officer by bugging him to assign me to the 1st Reconnaissance Battalion. While in the hospital, I met Lt. Chip Gregson, later Lt. General Gregson. He was recovering from a bullet wound in his heel he had gotten on a reconnaissance patrol. He extolled the virtues of being in the 1st Reconnaissance (Recon) Battalion. So, hoping that I wasn't making a major life-changing mistake, that was where I wanted to go. The personnel officer was busy, and not a little grumpy, with no time for a lowly second lieutenant, but I kept knocking on his door and reminding him of my request.

My persistence paid off. I am assigned to Charlie Company, 1st Recon Battalion. Jean Fitzsimmons, a buddy from The Basic School, is in Echo Company. Fitz, a North

Carolinian and former high school wrestler, had great enthusiasm for the Marine Corps and life in general. This made him popular at The Basic School.

Recon, when in the rear, sure has it better than what I saw in the infantry. Here at Camp Reasoner, Recon Battalion headquarters, we live in nice, dry hooches made of plywood with metal roofs. Inside, we have cots, covered by mosquito nets, and footlockers. We are right next to the 1st Marine Division headquarters and have access to the Da Nang PX, the biggest in the world. We have a refrigerator in the hooch, electric lights, and shower facility with hot water, everything except flush toilets. Relatively speaking, I am in heaven!

I was assigned as the platoon commander of the first platoon. I already have a mission. On December 6, I go out to the OP with two squads from my platoon.

Three observation posts are manned by elements, usually a platoon or less, of three companies in the battalion. Charlie Company's OP is situated on a mountain, overlooking a trail frequently used by enemy soldiers in the Que Son Valley. Each of the three platoons in the company rotates sending men to the OP for about a ten-day period.

December 11, 1969

It rained every day of the four I have been here. Yesterday, I took out a short patrol to look around our OP. We didn't see much, but we did get soaked to the skin. It rained in torrents. My boots still haven't dried out. It is cold at night. Fitzsimmons brought his team into our OP to be extracted. He looked like a drowned rat! His team had been inserted in the Que Son Mountains to look for General Giap. Supposedly, intelligence had placed him somewhere in the Que Son Mountains. At any rate, all Fitz's team got was wet. I gave him my poncho and poncho liner, and I slept in an old blanket. I was freezing!

I usually go out and check the sentries around 8 p.m., between 10 p.m. and 12 a.m., at 1:30 a.m., and at 3 a.m. I can't say I accomplish anything by checking the lines. It is too spooky up here for anyone to go to sleep on watch especially when the fog rolls in, but it makes me feel better and lets the men on watch know they haven't been forgotten.

My platoon provides security for the artillery team, one officer and three young Marines. Actually, I have two squads up here, seventeen men, including the four-man artillery team. Quarters are tight on this small mountaintop. One of my squads is back in the Recon Battalion area or on patrol. In recon, a squad is called a team. So I have three teams in my platoon. Each team consists of eleven men, although usually only six or seven go on patrol. A recon patrol consists of a point man, team leader, primary radioman, corpsman, man who carries the M79, assistant team leader, and tail end charlie. We move through the jungle more or less in that order.

The Marines have some kind of operation going on around here. They have set up a fire support base on a mountain near us. A fire support base consists of an artillery unit with an infantry unit to protect them.

December 12, 1969

I hold classes on the OP. We have a lot of time, and everyone can use some brushing up. Yesterday, the corpsman held a class on first aid, followed by a class on the quick-kill method of shooting, and some practice. I definitely needed the practice. Quick-kill is a point-to-shoot method for chance encounters. That is exactly what we normally face on a reconnaissance mission.

We had another class on shooting today. We have a daily routine. Time can hang heavy. In the mornings, we hold a police call, picking up all of the trash, and the corpsman burns the shitter. That is a cut-off fifty-five-gallon barrel with a toilet seat over it. The head (toilet) is next to the trash pit just outside our OP on the cliff side. There is no such thing as privacy.

I try to schedule at least one class a day, usually in the mornings. The afternoons and evenings when not on watch, the troops spend time playing cards, reading (xxx-rated books or magazines are big), or cooking up a meal. Before they come to the OP, they visit the PX and stock up on all sorts of ingredients they get together and share. They can be very inventive in the creation of their meals.

The artillery people finally got to fire last night. We only sighted fifteen NVA, and the artillery people credited themselves with killing five. In reality, it is very difficult to tell whether or not anyone is hit or how many we killed.

December 13, 1969

We sighted about forty NVA last night and killed about sixteen, or at least that was the estimate. It is all very impersonal. Through our binoculars we see these little figures walking down the trail in the valley. We call the artillery battery firing for us.

"Report Card Mike, this is Sandhurst. Over."

"Sandhurst, this is Report Card Mike. Over."

"Fire mission. Forty NVA at coordinates 983472. One round, will adjust. Over."

"Roger that, Sandhurst."

"Sandhurst, this is Report Card Mike. Shot out."

If the artillery round lands off the target.

"Report Card Mike, this is Sandhurst. Drop two hundred."

Next round lands on the target.

"Report Card Mike, this is Sandhurst. Fire for effect."

"Roger, Sandhurst."

"Shot out."

The whole battery fires. The figures on the trail disappear in a cloud of smoke and fire.

"Report Card Mike, this is Sandhurst. Over."

"Sandhurst, this is Report Card Mike. Over."

"Good coverage of target. Sixteen confirmed KIAs. Sandhurst out."

Sometimes there are bodies left on the trail, but normally the bodies disappear with the coming of dawn. The NVA never leave bodies if they can help it. They want to bury their dead, I am sure. They also do not want us to be able to confirm the actual number of KIAs we inflict.

December 14, 1969

We expect a resupply helicopter today. It probably will be a CH46. We get flipped, my platoon comes in, and the other platoon leaves with a CH53. It is a much bigger helicopter that can carry a heavier load. The troops bring plenty of food with them. I believe they wouldn't miss a meal even if we didn't have C-Rations. They have hamburgers, shrimp, weenies, sardines, corned beef, and I don't know what else.

We sighted over sixty NVA on the trail. Our artillery team, Sandhurst, called the artillery battery firing for us and gave them the exact range and coordinates of the enemy. The battery rained fire on the enemy. I would hate to have been under the barrage. Smoke from the explosions obscured our vision. We estimated we kill twenty of them, but it could have been more. The smoke and darkness ended our mission and made it impossible to get accurate figures.

I think most of the NVA we have seen are rice humpers, meaning their specific job is to carry rice to the fighting troops. They generally load up their packs with nothing but rice. That is how their supply line works. Infantrymen usually accompany them for protection.

At dusk, these NVA leave the mountains to the southwest of us and go northeast to the villages to collect rice and then return to the mountains before dawn. It usually is overcast, no light from the moon or stars. Consequently, we can't see them returning to the mountains, although we kill a bunch of them in the evenings as they go to the villages.

December 15, 1969

Last night, we sighted fifty-eight NVA. We couldn't tell how many we killed because the fog rolled in as we were shooting our mission.

It was a scary night. When the fog rolls in, there is no visibility. Sentries can't even see one another or from one end of the small bunker complex to the other end. We heard all kinds of noise outside the barbed wire surrounding us, cans rolling down the hill, and stuff like that. Apparently, the rats found a real delicacy outside the wire, and every rat in the area was rushing for his share. Of course, we couldn't tell what was making the noise. For all we knew, we were being probed by NVA. All we heard were the cans rattling around. We threw frags (hand grenades) periodically through the night. These are the nights when it pays to have a dog on the OP. With the dog's sense of smell, they can provide some warning of an imminent attack.

It was the nosiest night since we arrived. The fire base near us fired their big guns and threw frags. Machine gun and rifle fire came from the valley below us in addition to the frags we were throwing. It really rattled one of our new kids. When anyone throws a frag or fires the M79, he is supposed to yell "Outgoing!" That way everyone knows we are not receiving fire. The new kid was pretty scared. He threw a frag up toward the other end of the OP and forgot to yell anything. After it exploded, he remembered he was supposed to yell something but forgot what he was supposed to yell. Instead, he yelled, "Incoming!" which meant we were receiving fire. The hair stood straight up on my head, I grabbed my rifle, and struggled to get our bunker door open. The artillery officer and I, feeling a little spooked, had jammed the bunker door closed earlier that night to make it harder for the enemy to toss a grenade into it. Fortunately, we got things straightened out without any more mishaps.

December 17, 1969

Finally we got off the OP. It was cloudy and rainy all day. The clouds lifted just enough for a helicopter to get in and get us get out. A hot shower sure felt good. It is still raining here but much warmer.

Weathered In

December 22, 1969

My patrol was canceled due to the weather. The helicopters haven't been able to fly in these weather conditions. It would have been exciting to say the least. A company commander of the Q84th VC Company Chieu Hoied, which means surrendered, and gave the location of his company. My mission was to find his company. But not only was the Q84th in the area but also VC district headquarters, the Twenty-Second Company of the Thirty-First Regiment, D8 Battery of the Thirty-First Regiment, the Twenty-Second Transportation Battalion, a hospital, and the Twenty-Second Receiving Company. Not the best mission for a new team leader.

The way the process works: The S3 (operations) issues a frag (fragmented) order that notifies the selected team of the upcoming patrol. The frag order gives the team all the vital information. The call signs in this case were melody time for the battalion and puppet show for my team. Call signs and radio frequencies are changed often. The coordinates of the team's haven, usually a six-grid area, in which the team must stay, and the nearest artillery battery's radio frequency and call sign. In addition, an intelligence report attached to the frag gives the team an idea of what to expect in terms of water, terrain, trails, possible observation posts, and helicopter landing zones. It also tells when and where the enemy was last sighted, in what numbers, and whether contact was made.

After receiving a frag, the team leader usually posts a warning order that alerts his team and tells them what equipment to assemble. Later, the team leader gives an oral and detailed five paragraph order (situation, mission, execution, administration/logistics, command/signal).

I required each member of my team to carry the following: gas mask, four to six canteens (more if there is no water in our haven), two bandages carried in the right hand trouser pocket, insect repellent, LSA (rifle lubricant) with brush for our rifles, Halazone tablets for water purification, salt tablets, bush gloves, poncho liner, rope with snap link, camouflage stick, rations for five or six days, three fragmentation grenades, one CS grenade, and eleven cartridge magazines. Most of us carried more ammunition.

I would divide among the team binoculars (usually carried on the back of the point man in front of me where I could easily reach them), smoke grenades, C-4 (explosives), strobe lights, flashlights, claymores (I usually carried one), pen flares, medical kit, compasses, radios, white phosphorus grenades (I carried one), signal mirrors, plastic handcuffs, and air panels.

In addition, I carry a PRC 93 radio, a compact emergency radio that pilots are issued to communicate in the event they are shot down. We were pretty weighted down. We also carried an M79 grenade launcher and rounds for it. It wasn't much good against the enemy in thick jungle, but shooting illumination rounds into the air would help an aerial observer locate the team in an emergency.

Most Recon Marines had their Ka-Bar taped to the suspender strap holding up their equipment on the side that covered their heart. It was sort of a superstition. Supposedly, a Ka-Bar saved a Marine's life by deflecting an enemy round. I carried my bayonet taped to my suspender strap. I felt it was to my advantage to be able to put the knife on the end of my rifle, if it came to that.

December 24, 1969

I have just finished physical training. Even in a combat zone we have to keep in shape and our recon image. After calisthenics, we run in formation down the road by our base. We do this in extreme heat with boots and sometimes flak jackets. It is no wonder recon is viewed with trepidation by others.

Except for everyone carrying a weapon, this area hardly seems like a combat zone. We have a lot of leisure time, a great indoor handball court, enlisted and officer clubs, and a movie every night. In fact, my company has even built a small swimming pool. This is luxury living, especially compared to LZ Ross or Baldy.

I got fragged yesterday for a patrol on the twenty-seventh. All three of my teams will be going out, so I have been running around trying to get everything squared away. I also got tabbed to head the company's contingent for Admiral McCain's reception. We wasted about an hour and a half for his five-minute incoherent right-wing speech. Bob Hope will be at Freedom Hill (the Da Nang PX) tomorrow. I don't think I will go. Too many people.

December 27, 1969

I have been waiting all morning to be inserted with my team. We were finally secured about 12:30 p.m. The birds quit flying because of the weather. Yesterday was busy. The day before a patrol, there is a lot to do. We distribute our C-Rations to each patrol member and get the ammo request in to ordinance. I give a patrol order to the team detailing what everyone is doing and what to expect. We then test fire our weapons. Afterwards we practice immediate action drills so everyone knows what to do if we run into the enemy. We also practice crossing a danger area, any open area on our patrol route. Then weapons and magazines are cleaned.

I put my patrol gear together the night before going out. I am a little superstitious about how I put it together. I want everything exactly in the same place each time. We are lucky to have ass packs held by our suspenders and hooked onto our pistol belt. They ride low on our back and that helps keep it from catching on vines as we move through the jungle. We also have long-range rations. They are pretty good. We just add water and an entrée is created. I think we owe much of our good gear to Lt. "Dog" Jones, our supply officer. He takes a truck and regularly raids a nearby army post for gear we do not have.

We have to be at the ammo bunker at 6 a.m. to draw our ordinance. About 7 a.m., the helicopter pilots arrive. There are four helicopters used for insertions: two CH46s and two Huey or Cobra gunships. One CH46 carries the team, and one CH46 flies backup in case the first helicopter goes down. The CH46s are escorted by two gun birds, either Huey or Cobra. The gun birds soften up the insert zone, hopefully exploding any booby traps, or they provide fire support if the team is met by the enemy. The helicopter carrying the team slowly spirals down into the LZ hoping that if the enemy is present, they will be unable to resist opening fire before the helicopter lands and the team gets on the ground.

Thwap, thwap, thwap, thwap. The drama begins with the early morning sound of helicopters approaching our landing zone. Pilots along with each team leader and assistant team leader scheduled for insertion that day meet in the operations room for the pre-mission briefing. The briefer stands at a plastic-covered map, occupying the front wall, pointer in his hand. The location of every operating team is marked on the map.

I listen as the briefer points to my assigned area. He tells the pilots where I have chosen to be inserted, indicating the kind of terrain in our LZ. He recommends the best approach and in what direction the pilots might expect enemy fire as well as where and when the enemy was last sited. The briefer notes the location of any friendly troops in the area as well as alternative LZs. Each team leader is given the order in which his team will be inserted. The key piece of information for me is finding out when I will be inserted. I already know all of the other information. I always want to go in early. Not only because there is less time to get nervous, but it gives me a whole day to move off my LZ if the enemy comes looking for us.

The helicopters' arrival, the tense atmosphere in the briefing room, the briefer standing by the large plastic covered map, the rapt attention of pilots and team leaders, the image of the seven of us camouflaged head to foot, dropping into dense enemy-controlled jungle is right out of a Hollywood movie. Only the stakes are far higher.

Next to the Recon LZ, a small shed opens onto the landing zone. There, the teams wait their turn to be inserted. Next to the shed is a head (toilet) that most team members visit as they wait to be inserted. Carved on a wall of the head, among other names, is the name of the only Marine I know who thought he would be killed and was killed. It was a little eerie to see that before boarding a helicopter and setting off on a mission. Of course, one of the keys to survival in combat is to be able to control your thoughts. You can't dwell on possibilities. For example, night in the jungle is pitch black, full of noises, scary. It would be easy to allow your imagination to run wild.

Morning is the best time to be inserted and late afternoon the worst because a team needs to move away from their insertion point quickly. Sometimes we do mock insertions to mask from the enemy the actual insertion LZ.

December 28, 1969

I am still not out on my patrol. The weather has been too bad to get in our LZ. Because of the rain, I don't think we will get in today either.

I had my camera and tried to get a picture of a sentry dog and his handler. They were going out with one of my teams, acting as a radio relay for another team. While I was maneuvering for a position to get the picture, I took my eye off the dog for a minute, and he charged over and bit me. Some reward for taking his picture! I didn't even get a good picture because he turned around to snarl at someone else as I pressed the shutter. The Marines give him a wide berth because he goes after anything that moves.

January 1, 1970

I spent New Year's Eve with my platoon up on the division defensive lines as the reaction platoon. At midnight, you could see pyrotechnics go off everywhere. Marines were firing, flares were going up. It was a major light show. The general had expressly forbidden it, so he is probably gnashing his teeth.

January 4, 1970

It is 5 a.m., and I am sitting in the company office on watch. We were rolled out of bed at 1:30 a.m. and put on 100 percent alert. I dragged all of my gear down to the company office (and I had plenty of gear since I am supposed to leave on patrol today) plus my flak jacket and helmet. When I got there, they set up a watch and sent us back to bed. It seems Marble Mountain took a lot of rockets, and the expectation was something would happen here. With hardly any sleep, I am going to be hurting if we leave today. The sky is pretty clear, so we may very well get out today.

The shells were going overhead all night. They sounded as if they would land right on top of us. In reality, we couldn't hear any of them land. They made a loud rushing noise accompanied by a high whistle as they passed overhead.

One of the other lieutenants took a dog team to our OP. The company has two dog teams. The dog turned on the handler and chewed him up pretty badly. The handler only had that dog about a week. A special dog-handling team was sent to the OP to remove the dog. The handler was medevaced.[1]

January 8, 1970

I just got back from my first patrol. The weather let up just enough for the helicopters to fly. Our operating area was called Happy Valley. A misnomer, no doubt.

I was a little nervous as the helicopter spiraled down into a sea of tall elephant grass. The helicopter ramp dropped while the helicopter hovered. The crew chief motioned for us to get off. The helicopter wasn't stable, and I couldn't see the ground. I motioned to the crew chief to get the helicopter on the ground. The noise of the helicopter prohibited any real conversations. The crew chief was adamant. The pilots weren't going to land the aircraft.

We jumped. We each carried a heavy load of equipment. I was concerned that jumping any distance to the ground risked serious injury. Fortunately, it didn't happen.

---

[1] None of the dogs who served faithfully in Vietnam were brought home. They were euthanized, given away, or abandoned.

We hit the ground. Immediately, wet elephant grass closed over us, soaking us to the bone. The rain started again.

I got a radio check with the pilots to insure our radios were working. They also gave me the map location of our insert zone. I wasted no time in getting away from our landing zone. I wanted to be nowhere around if the enemy came looking for us.

A couple of hours into the patrol, we took a break. I sat down and pulled out my map. It dawned on me that I had no idea where we were. I failed to note the direction we had traveled from our LZ. There were no terrain features to shoot an azimuth and get a compass bearing. We were surrounded by elephant grass, limiting our vision to just a few feet.

The Marine Corps teaches new lieutenants to rely on their NCOs (noncommissioned officers), so I huddled with my assistant team leader.

Pointing at my map, I asked, "Where would you put us, Sergeant?"

"Shit, Lieutenant, I don't know." Not much help!

We remained lost for the entire patrol. It was a good thing we didn't run into trouble. I asked for an observation plane to over fly us, but the S3 responded by saying, "How the hell can you be lost? It's a valley. There's nothing but elephant grass!" Of course, there was nothing to take a compass bearing on either.

We crossed a stream that provided a few scary moments. It continued to rain, so the water in the stream was moving very fast. It was deeper than I expected. I went across first because I didn't want to take a chance of any of my men drowning. I got halfway across, and I started to worry I might drown. The footing was extremely uneven and slippery. The current was so strong that if I lost my footing, I would have gone under and been washed downstream before anyone could help me. With all the gear we carry, I wouldn't stand a chance.

We fixed up a rope for the rest of the men to hang onto when they crossed. We each carry a twelve-foot section of rope with a snap link. Next time, I will have enough sense to put a rope around me first so if I do slip, I can be dragged back. With wet, cold, chaffed hands, we clung to the rope, hoping the weight of our sodden equipment would not cause us to lose our grip and be swept away. It was a precarious, tense crossing. One man dropped his rifle and only by luck recovered it.

The foliage was thick. At times, we were on all fours, crawling through the bushes. In some places, if my point man got more than ten or twelve feet from me, I couldn't see him. One big difference from the infantry is that I stay right up behind the point man rather than letting him get well ahead. The second man frequently is the one to react to enemy contact while the point man is breaking a trail.

We got to the extract point and were extended a day. We were in a large valley covered with elephant grass that grew to heights well above our heads. There was nowhere to go for cover, so when moving to our harbor site, we spiraled into it on the theory that we would hear the enemy and have some warning if we were being trailed. The rain stopped long enough for us to be extracted. We popped a smoke grenade that the helicopter pilots had no trouble identifying, and we hauled our wet, shivering bodies out of the bush and onto our ride home.

Hill 425

January 10, 1970

I have been running around today like a headless chicken, trying to get everything ready for the OP. We are scheduled to be out fourteen days. I had to get my personnel roster made out, my ammo request in, and the rations we would need. I finally got all that done. My platoon sergeant is in the hospital with an ulcer, one of my team leaders is going on R & R, and the other is on light duty, so I didn't have much help. I also went to see the S1 (personnel) about an R & R date. Rest and relaxation is a week's leave everyone gets while in Vietnam. Married guys generally meet their wives in Hawaii, and single guys go to Australia, Thailand, or Formosa. Originally, I was told that all the dates for February were full. However, the S1 called and told me the first sergeant had given me his quota.

Jan. 12, 1970

About 4 p.m., we were inserted into the OP via CH53 helicopter. We brought all our gear as well as food and water, so we were loaded down. We settled into our bunkers. At 7:14 p.m., we sighted twelve NVA wearing green utilities and carrying packs and rifles. The artillery team called a fire mission with excellent coverage of the target. The result was six NVA confirmed KIA.

January 13, 1970

At 7:40 a.m., we observed four of the enemy, wearing black pajamas and carrying bags, packs, and rifles, and sitting on a bunker. We called a fire mission with good results: one KIA confirmed. 10:25 a.m., we spotted a VC, wearing black pajamas, carrying a pack, and sitting near a hooch. We called a fire mission, but the VC moved out of the area before the rounds impacted. At 5:45 p.m., eleven NVA, wearing green utilities with packs and rifles were observed. We called a fire mission, but it got too dark to see the results.

January 14, 1970

First thing this morning, twenty VC/NVA were spotted, going into a bunker. The artillery team called a fire mission, resulting in six KIAs. At 1:30 p.m. and at 4:15 p.m., more NVA were observed entering a bunker. The results of the first fire mission were obscured by fog. The second fire mission resulted in the destruction of the bunker. At 7 p.m., twenty-one NVA were sighted, moving on the trail in the valley. A fire mission was called, resulting in six KIAs. It was a busy day for the artillery spotters, and the batteries firing for them. The trail in the Que Son Valley is a major transit point. Most of our fire missions are directed there. Generally, every evening as it is getting dark, the VC/NVA start down the trail. And every evening we shoot them.

We have a daily routine. We get up in the morning and police the area first thing. Then we start filling sandbags. We are strengthening the walls and the bunkers. We work until about 1 p.m. Sometimes in the afternoons, we run short patrols around our position to look for any signs of the enemy nosing around. Two sentries at each end of the OP go on duty at 6 p.m. with all of their fighting gear (i.e., flak jacket, helmet, rifle, magazines, and gas mask). Everyone turns out at 6:30 p.m. with all of their gear and stands at their fighting position. This signals that we are getting serious about getting through the night. It also makes sure no one has mislaid their gear so they can't find it in an emergency. We practice every night to eliminate the chance of confusion should we get hit. Some nights we have a "mad moment" when everyone fires his weapon.

At night we have two men at either end of the OP on guard and a dog that periodically checks the wire, the same dog that bit me. We have called a temporary truce.

Our dog is something else. His name is Max, a beautiful German Shepherd. The first thing he did when he got up here was nip two people. After that, he had everyone squared away. He is the only one here who can urinate in the compound without anyone saying anything. If we are cooking, and he wants some, he just walks over and helps himself. As yet, no one has had the courage to tell him that it just isn't proper manners. One young Marine was walking to the other end of the bunkers with a sandwich in his hand. Max walked up, took a sniff, and let out a low growl. The Marine immediately surrendered the sandwich to Max, figuring discretion was the better part of valor. When Max is napping on one of the paths between bunkers, we detour, going the long way around. Actually, after the first day, Max hasn't had to resort to such low forms of coercion as growling. He just gives us the eye, and we become quite cooperative.

The first day was kind of funny. The dog handler put Max in a bunker and went back to the LZ for his gear. We were all standing around the bunkers and out came Max. Everyone started scurrying for the highest point they could find, me included, and yelling for the dog handler. You could mark Max's progress through the bunker complex by the Marines jumping for the top of the bunkers. It looked like pop goes the weasel. That was when Max realized he had us pretty well shaped up. He bit me before we came and nipped the corporal the first day. That left him unchallenged for command of the OP.

There are still a lot of NVA in the valley. We spotted twenty-one last night. Unfortunately, the fire support base next to us was moved. We don't get artillery quite as quickly and accurately as we used to. The artillery spotters are champing at the bit for the weather to clear so they can get off the hill for a ten-day R & R. We are dependent on good weather so the helicopters can fly.

We got word that we will have brass visiting the OP tomorrow. One of the VIPs may be the commanding general of the 1st Marine Division. Our artillery spotter setup has hit it off big with all the brass. It is called an IOD (integrated observation device). This top-secret device consists of very powerful binoculars, a laser range finder, and a NOD (night observation device), which provides some vision after dark. The artillery people are up for a bunch of medals for calling in artillery on the enemy. The team on our OP has around 150 confirmed kills.

January 21, 1970

It is colder than the devil, but it hasn't rained as much this time as last time I was here. A lieutenant from division came up yesterday to see about installing some listening devices for us. I am all for it. Every little thing helps us. We already have seismic devices planted to warn us of movement in any area where the devices were dropped by aircraft. I guess they really expect TET to be big this year. They (some unit at division) captured an enemy soldier who had a detailed overlay of Da Nang, supposedly a major target. The OPs manned by Recon Battalion are other suspected targets. That is why so many patrols are being run off of them. The big question is whether the enemy has enough strength left to hit Da Nang.

The patrol that ran off of our hill the other day has sighted thirty to forty NVA and a base camp not too far from us. I hope they don't pay us a visit. I think we would be all right if they did. This OP has gone very smoothly so far. Everyone has cooperated. The nights have been really clear for the most part, and with two people on watch at each end, I sleep pretty well.

January 23, 1970

The battalion CO who visited us is being medevaced to the US. He was nosing around at another OP with the lieutenant in charge. The lieutenant tripped a booby trap. The colonel apparently will be okay. The lieutenant lost his leg below the knee, his hand, and one eye.

A lot of enemy activity surrounds us. We are still shooting them in the valley and running air strikes in the mountains behind us. The recon team that went into the mountains found all kinds of NVA. The battalion S3 (planning) wants to send the team back in, but they are less than eager to go.

Report Card

January 28, 1970

Back from the OP. I have been fragged to lead a patrol going out January 30 to February 3. Things have been kind of rough here since I came back from the OP. I am glad I am going out. Bill Fairwell, a guy I met in the hospital who had a really messed-up hand, wrote and told me they cut off some of his fingers. He was an infantry platoon leader. He hit a booby trap on an operation. He had his hand out and his flak vest unbuttoned, very common in the heat. His hand and chest not protected by the vest caught the blast.

February 4, 1970

My last patrol wasn't too bad, a little cold but at least not wet. We were set up on a ridge, observing a river. We saw a few NVA with packs passing through the villages in the valleys on either side of us. I couldn't see calling artillery and blowing away the villages, women with children, and all in order to kill four or five NVA. Several of the NVA we observed moved out of the area before we could call a fire mission. I did call in artillery as the NVA crossed the river. However, I couldn't get it adjusted right. It either landed on the other side of the gorge or near us. At one time, we had shrapnel flying over our heads while the NVA we were shooting were a good one thousand meters away. I wanted the battery to fire a high-angle projection, but they were reluctant.

We did have a little excitement. We had harbored up for the night just off the trail running the length of the ridge. A harbor site is a concealed area, hopefully defensible, where a team hides for the night. I had a seven-man team. We slept close together, within an arms distance of the man on either side, as we always did when we harbored for the night. I kept a man on watch on either end of the harbor site.

It was pitch black like only a night in Vietnam could be. You literally could not see your hand in front of your face, much less the other end of the harbor site. I heard a rustling of bushes. I thought one of the new people had gotten up to relieve himself. A cardinal rule: one never moves around in a harbor site without first notifying everyone else. Otherwise, you could get shot by mistake.

I became increasingly agitated! The Marine on watch wouldn't answer his radio. We carry two. I began whispering loudly, trying to find out what dumb son of a bitch was moving around. No one answered. I became even angrier and louder. After about the third time I asked, and was about to get up and see for myself, a tiny, breathless voice came over the radio handset, "Someone just walked two feet in front of me."

Needless to say, all the hair on my head stood on end. By some stroke of luck, the NVA walked two feet from our harbor site and didn't see or hear us.

If that wasn't enough to keep us awake, something, it must have been one of the mysterious rock apes, came around. It rattled rocks, cans (other teams had left their trash), bushes, and everything else all night long. We were expecting a horde of NVA soldiers to break upon us any moment. Nights in the bush are scary even at the best of times.

One night, the boredom of standing radio watch was broken by a blow-by-blow account from an OP being hit by the enemy. The lieutenant on the radio described how the NVA were taking off their clothes and repeatedly charging his wire to be mowed down by his men. He was sustaining no casualties while he was inflicting numerous casualties upon the NVA. It was very entertaining to hear the battle described over the radio. As it turned out, battalion sent a reaction team out the next day. They found no bodies and no blood trails. It seems the lieutenant and his crew, heavily into dope, invented or imagined it all. That was the end of that lieutenant in the battalion.

Another night while listening to the radio, a recon team had a tiger carry off one of its members from their harbor site. There was a good deal of radio traffic from the team, trying to figure out what had happened. It was pitch black, and they couldn't see anything. They found their mauled team member dead the next day. Like many other teams, the team only had one person on watch at night. One more reason to keep two people on watch.

The jungle is a dangerous place! Numerous people living there are trying to kill us as well a significant variety of vary poisonous snakes and tigers who may or may not have had a taste of human blood. Some teams have reported seeing elephants, although they haven't presented a threat to any team.

I have done a little remodeling in the cubbyhole where I sleep. I built a rickety little table with a rickety little chair to go in one corner so I would have something to write on. I turned my cot sideways and got rid of a big box. I made a table out of it. All of the company officers sleep in the same hooch. We each create a little space for ourselves, sometimes even putting up plywood dividers.

February 20, 1970

We are in our training cycle. It has been busy, and I have been dead tired at night. Today, we went to an artillery range for classes on calling in artillery. Yesterday, we practiced on the SPIE rig, a method of inserting or extracting a team in an area where a helicopter cannot land. That was scary!

The helicopter extends a long nylon line from its belly. Marines wait below in something like a parachute harness with their rope threaded through D rings in the shoulders of their harness. Another D ring is attached to the rope. The line from the helicopter has various points where Marines hook their D ring. The helicopters gain altitude with Marines dangling below held to the nylon line by the rope on their harness. I think helicopter pilots take great glee in going as high as they can with us dangling below. The sights are great, if only I weren't thinking about my knot slipping, or the rope breaking.

Tomorrow, I will escort a USO show from Da Nang to Recon Battalion. Most of the shows we get come from the Philippines. The drive from Da Nang to 1st Recon is full of interesting sights and sounds. The road is clogged with vehicles. Mopeds, sometimes with the whole family aboard, weave in and around bigger vehicles. Pedestrians walk, talk, hawk various wares, or just sit and watch traffic, line the side of the road. A warren of rickety buildings and lean-tos known to Marines as dog patch border each side of the road. Little shops and bars face the road, offering their services. Virtually anything one can imagine goes on there, including prostitutes and dope. Deserters and AWOL (absent without leave) Marines hide out there as well.

After R& R, it was really tough, leaving Red, getting on the airplane in Hawaii, and coming back to Vietnam. Hawaii was a pleasant interlude where I didn't have to worry about getting shot, blown up, or eaten by a tiger. The week went way too fast. I moped the whole way back. Predictably, some returning Marine stood up in the airplane, pointed to the new guys coming to Vietnam, and sang out, "Some of you won't be coming *baaack*." You can always count on there being a jerk in any situation. It was a subdued group.

Now that I am back, I feel much better. I thoroughly enjoy my platoon.

The esprit de corps is very high in 1st Recon. That is not surprising when the unit is all about putting six- or seven-man teams into enemy-infested jungle. We could not operate effectively without that esprit de corps. The high morale makes the transition from R & R back to my unit much easier.

7

Casualties

March 1, 1970

A man from Charlie Company was killed and another wounded. The company won't tell us who they are. I have a suspicion it was our company commander. He apparently was being lifted out of the jungle on the jungle penetrator, a device helicopters lower into the jungle when they cannot land. The cable snapped at about six hundred feet. Our battalion tried to get a reaction team into the area the next day, but the NVA shot them out of the landing zone. I won't know the whole story until I get back. We were supposed to have an admin run today to bring in more supplies, but there were three emergency extractions, so we got left out.

Things have been fairly uneventful here on the OP. The night before I got here, the team sighted 150 NVA at the foot of the hill. So far, our largest sighting is fifty-six. It was so dark that we lost them and couldn't see the results of our artillery rounds. Roger Bullard, who was in my platoon in Officer Candidate School and The Basic School, is going to be the new artillery lieutenant on our OP. I was happy to see him. He says he heard that Alex Fitch is over here. Alex Fitch and I shared a common bond. He, like me, was older than most of the other lieutenants. When he was younger, he spent several years as a member of the 82nd Airborne Division. So, like me, he didn't have to be in the military. We were both married, and we joined the Marine Corps to go to Vietnam for somewhat altruistic reasons.

Roger turned out to be a short-term bunker mate though. When a rat jumped in bed with him one night, with a startling whoop, he went flying out the door. Rain or shine, he refused to spend another night in our bunker.

March 7, 1970

We have two more days until we get off the OP. We lost our company commander and a new lieutenant in our company. I don't know the full story, but apparently the new lieutenant, Lt. Skibbie, was wounded on a patrol. When the team was emergency extracted, he fell off of the ladder. The company commander, Captain McVey, must have gone out with the reaction team. As darkness descended, he asked to be lowered by jungle penetrator to find the body. It was getting too dark, he hadn't found the body, and he was being brought back into the helicopter. The safety officer in the helicopter took Captain McVey's rifle, put it down, and when he turned back, the captain was gone. The cable on the penetrator snapped at about six hundred feet.

The next day another reaction team was sent out to find both bodies, but they were shot out by the enemy, meaning they started taking enemy fire before the helicopters could land. Yesterday, a bigger reaction team was sent in. The NVA shot down a helicopter and pinned down the team. Last we heard, there were twenty-two wounded, and they were trying to get medical supplies into our forces.

The downed chopper had grunts (infantrymen) in it, probably ARVN (Army of the Republic of Vietnam). A recon team with the ARVN units, led by Lt. Polster of Charlie Company, was sent to report to battalion on the progress of the mission. The bodies of Lt. Skibbie and Captain McVey still hadn't been recovered[2]. The area was very hot with units taking lots of fire and casualties. The recon team was right in the middle of it. The colonel was furious because he was not getting more regular reports from the team.

In a separate incident, another lieutenant from recon was killed on the jungle penetrator. That represents three people killed in two months because a jungle penetrator broke! Needless to say, I will fix bayonets before I climb on that thing! The lieutenant was from the 3 shop (battalion planning). He volunteered to recover the body of an aviator who had flown into a ridge. The speculation is the aviator became so fixated on his target, he did not pull out of his dive until it was too late. Apparently, it is not an unheard-of phenomenon. The bottom line: it cost two lives.

---

[2] To my knowledge, the bodies were never recovered.

I never really think about being killed. I know it is a possibility, but I guess, like most people, I think of it in terms of someone else, not me. For that matter, I seldom get nervous the night before a patrol. I simply do not let my mind go there. In some respects at least, I have always been lucky. And war, as much as anything else, is a matter of pure luck. Of course, I hedge all of my bets by trying to take the element of luck out of the equation. But even if you are a wonderful person, a great family member, devoted to your religion, really good at what you do, the bottom line is it makes no difference if you are in the wrong place at the wrong time. Death is a random affair. All casualties are a waste of life, but it seems doubly so for those who are killed in accidents or equipment failure.

March 10, 1970

I am still on the OP. Actually, it is a party every night, held by, and exclusively for, the rats! At night they come out by the millions, a conservative estimate no doubt. I sleep with my face covered and rat stick by my side that I use to thrust, parry, and slash at the rats. Some of these rats are as big as hamsters. Now that our sentry dog is gone, I don't know if I am more leery of the rats or the NVA. Of course, with the dog here, there is no question in my mind. I am more leery of the dog.

March 17, 1970

I am back from the OP and sitting in the company office covered up in paper work. I am working on fitness reports, end-of-tour awards, and meritorious promotion write-ups. I also reorganized my platoon, changing team members and leaders around some. There hasn't seemed to be much bitching about it at all, which surprises me. Maybe I just haven't heard it.

Tomorrow, I am taking out another team. My call sign, pony boy, is at least a change from my other patrols where my call sign was report card. I like pony boy better. My academic record being what it was, report card didn't have a very positive connotation.

I went down to the prebriefing this morning to see about a visual reconnaissance of my haven. So many teams are either going out or coming in it very unlikely I will get one. Too bad because with a visual reconnaissance, you fly over your haven and get an idea of what things on the ground look like. It helps with navigation when you actually get on the ground because bushes, trees, and hills make it hard to see prominent terrain features. In thick jungle, there is virtually no visibility. The team scheduled to go out today got shot out, so they will try tomorrow. A lot of teams have been shot out lately.

March 23, 1970

I am back and going out again! I got back about 4 p.m., the twenty-second, and I am scheduled to leave again on the twenty-fifth. All patrols have been made six days long. Six days of absolute silence and constant vigilance, and we are running one patrol right after another. In addition, the NVA are putting out anti-recon units. We have been having a lot of teams shot out of their insert LZs. We reuse some LZs mainly because there are no other landing zones in the area, so the NVA are posting LZ watchers on them. They are out hunting us. The infantry has pretty much avoided contact. We have become a large pain in Charlie's backside. In fact, Recon has had more confirmed kills by small arms in the last three or four months than the whole rest of the division.

Mike Curry at Charlie Company's OP. The Que
Son Valley is in the background.

1ˢᵗ Recon's LZ. Most of our patrols began here.

Entering Charlie Company's area

Hill 425, Charlie Company's OP. It was a small bunker complex on the crest of a mountain overlooking a busy NVA supply route.

I shared this bunker on our OP with the artillery officer, not to mention the rats.

Lt. Curry, tired and malodorous after six days in the jungle.

Except for the final day, my last patrol wasn't too bad. As usual, it rained like the devil the last day. The birds spent most of the day on weather hold. We figured we wouldn't get out on time. Luckily, at the last minute, they came. We were thoroughly wet and miserable. The terrain we moved through was unbelievable, full of wait-a-minute vines that catch on our equipment, and make movement painfully slow. The bushes were so thick, we sometimes had to crawl. By the end of our patrol, our uniforms were rotten, ripped, and rank! The jungle emits a fetid odor of wet decay that permeates everything.

We got two more people from my basic school class, Paul Eglevsky and Jim House, assigned to Recon. With Walters, Fitz, Hodgins, and me, we have six people from my basic school company. Nice to have familiar faces around.

March 24, 1970

Fitz went out today on a big platoon operation. Tomorrow, I have to get up about an hour earlier than normal because the battalion is trying to put in a radio relay team at dawn. Our insertion will be secondary to getting that team in. The battalion has Fitz and his company's platoon operation out there without good communications. That is a very dangerous situation.

Patty Shell

We spiraled down inviting any enemy soldiers in the area to open fire before we got off the helicopter. There was no LZ. The helicopter couldn't land. It backed into a shell hole and dropped the ramp. Only the ramp touched the ground as we exited, scrambling to the lip of the shell hole. The point first, me next, followed by my radioman, and the rest of the team forming a 180-degree arc. We took up firing positions, not knowing what to expect. The helicopter hesitated a minute in the event we did take fire, we could scramble back aboard. The insertion is when we are the most vulnerable. The enemy could be waiting. We have no idea. A shot rang out! Immediately, I thought, "They're shooting at us!" All my senses surged until my radioman let me know the shot came from him. It was an accident. He missed killing me by inches. Not an auspicious beginning.

We checked our communications, got our replot from the pilots, giving us our map location, and set off for the high ground. If we got into a firefight, I always wanted to be on the high ground. The whole area had been bombed out. We worked our way up to an old fire support base. Seeing no indication of the enemy, we reversed our course. I made a decision to walk through an open space rather than take a long circuitous route through the dense tangle of brush that resulted from the bombing.

Walking down the hill, we crossed a small steam into the jungle. No sooner had we stepped into the foliage than we spotted a base camp. Everyone froze. We silently watched the area. After a period of time, seeing no movement, I whispered to my radioman to pass the word that we would circle the base camp and enter it from high ground. Three of us—point man, radioman, and me—took off, circling the camp. Fortunately, the base camp was old and deserted. That was a relief, considering how exposed we had been, coming from the fire support base.

As we came back through the camp, I came face to face with Quaid. He had his rifle sighted on me and was squeezing the trigger. He had me dead in his sights. The only thing that saved me was the unusual-colored camouflage I had on my face that morning. Quaid recognized the camouflage and held his fire. Thank god! The radioman, already on my shit list for his accidental discharge, hadn't passed the word to those behind him. They were left wondering where we had gone. When we popped up in the base camp, it had given them a scare. Nothing like the scare Quaid gave me!

The relief was short lived. We walked right into another base camp. The first thing we saw was a table with a couple of half-eaten bowls of rice sitting on it. A pot of rice was on the fire. My hackles went up. Trying to look everywhere at once, we cautiously made our way through the camp, expecting to come face to face with the enemy at any moment. There were hooches with bunkers dug beneath them, a hospital, an eating area, a latrine with fresh feces, and a couple of old rifles. We searched the base camp and took whatever papers or drugs we found lying about. The enemy must have seen us coming and fled. Lucky for us, they weren't there in numbers or they were too sick to fight.

We could get no communication with Recon Battalion, or anyone else. We were on our own, just the seven of us in an area crawling with enemy soldiers.

We continued walking slowly, silently through the jungle, stopping regularly to listen for any sounds that might indicate enemy presence. Little sunlight filtered through the triple canopy overhead. It created a gloomy, cool, lush surrounding without heavy underbrush, making it easier to move quietly. Tension rose as we found more signs of the enemy. We had no radio communication. Our radio was our lifeline. If we made contact with the enemy, we could get no help. There were too few of us to survive a determined enemy attack. We would be dead men.

Over the next few days, we found well-used trails among other signs of enemy presence. Crossing one heavily traveled trail, we came to a stream. The ground beyond the stream sloped sharply up. We needed to get to some high ground in order to reestablish communications with the battalion. We also needed water. We crossed the stream, and the bulk of the team moved up the hill. I remained in the stream with the Marines providing security for the one filling our canteens. We stayed quiet, communicating through whispers or hand gestures. I glanced up to an open area about fifty meters above us in time to see an enemy soldier emerge from the jungle. We all hit the deck and froze. We were highly exposed lying in the stream. We counted on our camouflage to conceal us from the casual glance.

Not daring to move, I was tracking the enemy soldier with my rifle. Quaid, I think it was, whispered, "Shoot him, Lieutenant. Shoot him!" Then another enemy soldier emerged, and another, and another. At this point, Quaid whispered, "Don't shoot, Lieutenant. Don't shoot." I wasn't intending to shoot until I knew what we were dealing with. We could get no more than three at a time in the clearing, and we had no idea how many we couldn't see. We didn't want to shoot the three we could see and have a bunch behind them attack us. We were far too vulnerable. One of the enemy soldiers pointed in our direction. We remained still. Had he moved his rifle, we would have killed him. We counted seventeen enemy soldiers as they crossed the clearing. Actually, I counted significantly more than seventeen, but that may have reflected my surging adrenalin, so I went with the smaller number suggested by a team member.

As soon as they quit crossing, we scrambled up the hill where we could get communications. By the time I got an aerial observer (AO) on station, the enemy was long gone. We did, however, find a great ambush site along a heavily used trail. The one major problem with it was we still had no communications with battalion. I kept one radio operator who had contact with the battalion on the hill as a relay in the event we sprang the ambush. We set up in an ambush until it began to get dark and then moved off to find a harbor site.

When we finally made contact with the battalion, they wanted us to go back and burn the base camp that we had found. Well, there was no way I was going to do that! It would have taken us several days just to get to the base camp to say nothing of announcing our position to the enemy. Battalion kept us in place another day. They wanted to flip us with another team because it was difficult to find a secure LZ. The following day, the other team was inserted, and we were extracted. The bird couldn't land because of the terrain, so the other team jumped off, and we clambered up on the helicopter ramp as it hovered.

The team we flipped with walked the trail, ran into NVA, got into a firefight, and had to be extracted the day they were inserted. In our debriefing, I recommended the area be targeted for an arc light (B52s) bombing mission and that other teams should not be sent into the area because of the poor communication and lack of LZs.

April 2, 1970

I have another patrol April 6 to April 11, and we flip up to the OP on the twelfth. On my last patrol, I flipped with Paul Eglevesky. His team replaced mine in a secure LZ. So far, all of my patrols have been straight inserts, which means that my team is inserted into an unsecured landing zone. We never know beforehand what we will be facing when we are inserted.

I have a tough time getting a good night's sleep. Night before last, I was exhausted. In the middle of the night, we caught some rockets in the battalion area. All kinds of sirens went off, but the rockets weren't very close. Last night, we had a really good Australian floorshow. The staff officers club got wild. The colonel and virtually everyone else, but me, were drunk and up on the stage dancing. It was something to behold! A couple of the officers came into our sleeping hut about midnight, staggering drunk, and woke everyone up. Stump Baker, who would be our company commander, had the disconcerting habit of pulling out his .45, chambering a round, and putting it under his pillow. I slept each night in the hopes he would not see any pink elephants and start blazing away at them.

April 5, 1970

I have a patrol tomorrow, and we were told today we would be taking two ARVN rangers. It will be a pain! They don't speak English, so it will be a game of charades.

The OP and Back

April 12, 1970

I finally made it to the OP. These fourteen days are going to be like R & R. Out of the last thirty days, I have spent twenty in the bush on patrol. My last patrol was pretty easy. There were no NVA, and easy movement, but very hot!

We observed some NVA disappear into a bunker in the valley. My radioman said he had a FAC (forward air controller) on the net, asking for targets. FACs flying in small aircraft act as a liaison between the ground elements and aircraft because ground troops cannot communicate with strike aircraft. The radio frequencies are different.

I came up on the net, "Hotspot (his call sign), this is Sunrise (my call sign). Over."

"Sunrise, I have a couple of fast movers (jet aircraft) with ordinance to expend. Do you have any targets?"

"Hotspot, that's affirm." I gave the coordinates of the bunker. "The bunker is in those trees. Over."

"Roger that. Fast movers are on their way."

Seemingly out of nowhere, two jet aircraft zoomed in, releasing their bombs in the target area. Smoke from the bombs' explosions billowed up into the air.

"On target, Hotspot."

"Sunrise, we are going to make an insurance run at the target."

Again the jets zoomed in, releasing their ordinance. More explosions followed by billowing smoke.

"Sunrise, this is Hotspot. Our ordinance is expended. We are off."

"Great job, Hotspot. Thanks."

April 17, 1970

I have finally become a killer! I got two rats. Tonight, I am going for mass murder. I am going to have rattraps all over my bunker.

The infantry has been running operations around our OP. They haven't seen too much mainly because they don't go into the enemy stronghold, which is behind us. I suppose casualties would be too high. Recon goes in there all the time. Of course, the team usually ends up being emergency extracted after about the second day.

For some reason, my bunker smells just like a garbage dump. I don't know whether someone has been urinating off the top where the radio watch is again or not. It is an awesome responsibility to be responsible for thirty people, what they do, and what they don't do. What they do to each other and what happens to them. The running of the OP is a little slacker than the last time, and the understanding is "Don't ruin a good thing." My old people seem to be shaping up pretty well except for the 10 percent in every crowd. I have some new ones who are a little too "wise ass." I hope I can straighten them out quickly. They seem to be influenced by the 10 percent.

At night, everyone stands a two-hour watch with four hours off and two hours on again. Night is when we really get serious about the whole thing. Each night, we also have a three-man listening post (LP) for early warning that goes outside the wire one hundred to three hundred meters.

The other night, the LP spotted five enemy soldiers coming toward them. I wanted to slip the LP back in and put artillery on the enemy, but the team leader with the LP panicked. He ran all the way in, making all kinds of noise and leaving a claymore mine and a gas grenade out there. When we went back the next day, they were both gone. All I can do is pray the claymore isn't used against any Marines. It was very stupid to leave it, and I have to take responsibility because I should have had the team blow it if they couldn't retrieve it. As it was, the NVA knew where they were anyway because they had panicked and made all that noise getting back.

April 20, 1970

Today, one of the teams from our company is in contact. Something is always happening. I am giving a class on plotting artillery targets, calling in an AO, and a little on selecting an LZ. Before going out on patrol, we plot artillery targets around our prospective LZ. At night when we settle into our harbor site, we always plot targets around our position in case some NVA come nosing around in the middle of the night. In the pitch black of night, a reference point for quick-supporting fires comes in handy. My platoon is less than enthusiastic about these classes as they have had them before. Hopefully, the repetition will help them to really know it.

April 22, 1970

We spotted two VC, wearing black pajamas, carrying rifles and a light machine gun, and following a streambed. We brought our .50 caliber machine gun over and fired them up. It seems unlikely we hit either of them, unless we got them with a ricochet, but we certainly hurried them along on their journey.

April 30, 1970

Back from the OP. We have finished moving our stuff from our old hooch down to a hooch in the company area.

The "big wheels" around here insist officers live in the company area. Apparently, there is a problem with pot in the battalion and closer supervision by the officers is needed. I don't think it has been a problem in our company. I want to think that we were in a pretty elite unit, and none of us who regularly were in the bush would risk being under the influence of drugs. Too much was at stake in the bush. Any drug problem, with rare exceptions, resided with those in the rear with the gear. They may have too much time on their hands.

Our battalion commander has flipped over the edge! Last night, we had a USO show at our officers/non-commissioned officers club. The colonel showed up about half-way through. I was tempted to leave because last time he came, he got bombed and made a spectacle of himself. I should have left.

On the table reserved for the colonel was a skull with a knife through its teeth. The colonel got up on the stage and started a long eulogy about all the officers we are going to have killed in the next three to ten days and about all the ones he has already sent to their deaths. He also talked about how we should go out and meet our deaths like men, on our shields, the glory of going to Valhalla. He said he expected his lieutenants to take the first bullet. He ranted on and on about all the lieutenants he was going to send to their deaths. I couldn't believe a CO, or anyone else, would say that. I left as soon as I could.

The speech shocked everyone who heard it. One platoon commander left the club in tears. He had just had a man killed, and the speech hit too close to home. Speaking for me, I was not planning on visiting Valhalla anytime in the near future, and I had no interest in taking the first bullet, or any bullet thereafter!

Some of these young Marines really have problems. I have one Marine whose parents are divorced. His mother has leukemia with a matter of weeks to live. He could go home, but he is willing to stick it out here. Another Marine just got word today that his father has terminal cancer and only months to live. They are both good men.

I had Officer of the Day Tuesday. The officer of the day is rotated among the officers in the battalion. The officer of the day handles all the relatively minor problems that arise during his twenty-four-hour tour of duty. Until Tuesday, I had never written anyone up (referred disciplinary charges). Tuesday night, I wrote up two Marines: one for sleeping on post and one for not standing his post properly. They both will go to the battalion commander. One of our guard posts is on a road leading into the battalion. Next to it is a culvert. After dark, whores, whose teeth are nonexistent, or black with betel nut, show up and entertain paying customers. They throw a blanket down in the culvert and set up for business. Venereal disease runs rampant. Even so, they have plenty of business from eager young Marines. It is probably a good thing for the customers that most nights are very dark.

I have gotten fragged for the fifth. We will be going into a pretty busy area. It is near the Thong Duc Special Forces Camp, now under siege. It ought to be exciting. I have 108 days left!

8

Veal Stew

May 10, 1970

I just got back and am going out again on the thir-teenth. My patrol had some exciting moments. I was staged, along with two other teams, at An Hoa Fire Support Base while the helicopters inserted us in turns. The birds usually take only one team at a time even though there are always two transport helicopters, CH46s. One bird is always kept empty to use for recovery in case the other goes down. In this climate, the helicopters have to be very careful about the amount of weight they carry.

While we were waiting, one of my platoon's teams inserted before us, which had been on the ground about for thirty minutes, got into contact. The radioman was shot in the back. It got his liver and bladder. I asked to go with the medevac but was refused. Not much of a beginning. On top of that, neither of my radios worked. A panic ensued, and two new radios were flown out to us from Recon.

We boarded the bird. When we got to our haven, we could find no LZs. We were put down next to a river outside our haven. As usual, the gun birds gave us the wrong replot. Consequently, we didn't know exactly where we were. It is virtually impossible to navigate in the jungle unless you know your starting point on the map. It was the thickest terrain I had seen. The point, a new man, took a couple of steps, tentatively parted some of the foliage, turned to me, and said, "We can't go here, Lieutenant!" I ended up walking point. I walked fifty meters, fought is the word, was covered in sweat, and had finished two-and-a-half canteens of water. The terrain and the heat were incredible! We did our best to move away from the LZ as quickly as possible, but with the terrain and the heat, we didn't get very far. We got an AO out to us, and he gave us our correct position.

That night, as we were settling into our harbor site, the battalion came over the radio saying two hundred NVA were spotted near our insert LZ, about four hundred meters from where we were harbored up. Battalion told us that our position had been compromised and ordered us to quickly move as far away as possible. With the terrain being what it was, it would have been impossible in the daylight, much less after dark. Besides, we were exhausted. As it turned out, the Da Nang DSAC had gotten excited about the two hundred NVA and had passed the grid coordinates of our position over the radio in the clear (not coded). The enemy monitors our radio nets. Consequently, the location of all teams is supposed to be given in code. Calling our coordinates in the clear had compromised our position. Fortunately for us, the enemy didn't do anything about it.

We spent the rest of the patrol within our haven looking for the NVA who were shooting rockets into the Thong Duc Special Forces Camp. Two evenings in a row, the NVA sent rockets into Thong Duc from a position about one thousand meters from us. In the relative quiet of the jungle, the unexpected whoosh of those rockets made us jump! I should note that the jungle really is never quiet, especially at night. We tried to get a fix on the launching points and report it to battalion. However, the jungle was too thick to see anything, so we had to work by sound. In addition, periodically throughout the day, there were single rifle shots, sometimes with answering shots. That was one way the NVA signaled each other. We didn't know whether the shots represented NVA out hunting us or not.

Walking point, I slid through the bushes and under the vines. Wait-a-minute vines caught on all our equipment. I began to duck under a vine, thought better of it, stepped back, and prodded it with my rifle. It slithered off. I have never been overly fond of snakes and that gave me something to think about when ducking under other vines along the route.

We had a real hassle getting out. The 3 shop wouldn't clear us to go back to our insert LZ, and there were no other LZs. We were stuck! The day we were extracted, the 3 shop finally cleared us to return to our insert LZ. We were nowhere near it. The jungle was far too dense, and our time too short to consider breaking a path. I chose to move on low ground in a shallow river that provided few obstacles as the quickest way to get to our extract point. We were taking a big chance, but I didn't see any good options. Two hundred of the enemy had been sighted on our extract LZ, rockets were being launched from an overlooking hill, and there had been signaling rifle shots throughout the area. I was walking point and a little anxious to say the least. I had an AO fly cover for us until he ran low on fuel, then the gun birds covered us the rest of the way. We humped our fannies off to get there! Fortunately, the enemy wasn't waiting in force. We did take some small arms fire as we were being extracted.

When we got back to the battalion area, the new man on the team found a bullet hole in one of his magazine pouches. He had fallen while running for the helicopter. Apparently, that was why. Before our patrol, he had turned down a compassionate transfer due to the ill health of his mother. After our patrol, he wasted no time reapplying for the transfer and left in short order. The patrol, apparently, gave him a reality check.

May 14, 1970

We were put in on a ridge on the Hai Van Pass in the Annamite Mountain Range on a wet, cold, blistery day. Our intelligence brief indicated numerous enemy base camps in the area. Previously, a recon team had been wiped out somewhere in this area. We were dependent on a radio relay for our communication with the battalion. There were no LZs in the area except the one where we were inserted.

While moving through our haven we saw a bamboo viper lying on a rock shelf. We gave him wide berth. Later, while sitting down taking a break, I saw another viper curled up a couple of feet from me. It was a short break! We decamped immediately and moved on. We saw a total of four bamboo vipers. They are known as the three-step snake because after being bitten that is about all the time the victim has before death. That night in our harbor site, we took extra care rolling up in our poncho liners to ensure we had no unwanted guests.

Other than the vipers, it was an uneventful patrol. Eventually, we moved back to our insert LZ to await extraction. We were miserable, wet clear through, and shivering in the cold. The sky was darkening, filled with ominous-looking clouds. The weather was a major concern as we waited anxiously for our turn to be extracted. Just as our turn came, the birds shut down. We were livid! We were convinced the pilots stopped for happy hour, but almost as bad, it seems that one of the teams had shot a tiger, and the pilots all wanted their picture taken with it. The dark rain clouds continued to close in. We had visions of another wet, miserable night. At the last minute, literally, before the weather made it impossible, the birds arrived, and we were extracted. It seems that our radio relay had been extracted, and they couldn't leave us in without communication.

Pathfinder

May 20, 1970

Yesterday wasn't a very good day for Charlie Company. One of our teams had a man shot in the chest and arm. He was medevaced. The rest of the team was extracted by ladder, and as they were being lifted out, the ladder hit a tree and knocked two men off of it. One was killed and the other seriously hurt. Another team had two men medevaced with temperatures of 103/104 degrees. Malaria.

I will be the company executive officer. I am doing that job now. The current XO is going home in a week. Mike Hodgins and I have the same date of rank, but for whatever reason, I ended up as the XO. I think it had to do with the relative position of our last names in the alphabet.

Yesterday, I went on a MEDCAP to two Vietnamese villages. A MEDCAP is a medical team that goes out to a village and sets up a clinic for the day. The villagers line up and wait patiently to see one of the medical personnel who clean infections, bandage wounds, give advice, issue medication, and generally provide what assistance they can. It is the only time many of the villagers get to see a doctor. One of the villages was extremely poor and shabby. The other was quite beautiful. My impression was that the MEDCAP was useful, but looking around the villages, I saw projects built by Americans that were not used by the villagers. That seemed a waste. The American builders apparently had a different set of priorities than the Vietnamese villagers. That is the story of this whole war, I'm sure.

May 26, 1970

I am sitting in the company office, pouring sweat. It seems that when I am in the bush, I am cold, and when I am in the company area, I am hot. I don't mind the heat, but I hate being cold and wet! Being XO is a lot of work. I do everything the CO doesn't want to do. I get all the busy work and errands. This week, I have to set up the guard, training, and reaction rosters, also the OD schedule. I have to see about memorial services for one of our guys, get the company ready for the battalion commander's inspection, and see that the platoon commanders are caught up on their paperwork. Most terrifying of all is eating breakfast with the colonel every morning our company commander is on patrol.

The company executive officer does not have a platoon. When missions come up, they are assigned to a platoon. That left me out of the loop. I had to seek opportunities to lead recon teams. Which I did.

I just got back from a pathfinder mission for the 7th Marines. We went in to secure an LZ for a battalion of the infantry. It turned out to be a little hairy. The LZ was on top of Hill 845 in the Que Son Mountains. There are lots of enemy soldiers in the Que Sons.

We were expendable! It was good tactics. The infantry didn't want to land in a booby trapped area, or be met by an enemy force intent on wiping them out with the resulting casualties! So we were sent. Losing seven Marines was a better trade-off than losing an infantry battalion. Well, it was a better trade-off for them! I wasn't enamored with the idea!

We were inserted right on the LZ we were to secure, a small dirt strip cut into the top of the mountain. We moved a short way from the LZ and stayed for the rest of the day. In the evening, we moved a little further and ate our meal while waiting for dusk. The Marine walking at the tail of the team, motioned to me. The man assigned to walk last spends the bulk of his time looking backward, making sure we are not followed. "Sir," he whispered, "I think we are being followed." I studied the area, but I couldn't see anyone behind us. I thought he might have a case of the nerves.

At dusk, we moved again and harbored up for the night. The second move, just before dark, is designed to obscure our exact location from the enemy if he is aware of our presence. It is standard operating procedure.

A powerful lightning storm rolled over us. The sky was alive! Bolts of lightning flashed followed by the deep rumble of thunder. Rain pelted us as we huddled in our small perimeter, laying on the sodden ground, water cascaded beneath us. Everything was soaking wet. We turned off the radios and dismantled the antennas. We were on high ground, and lightning has hit the radio antenna of more than one recon patrol, in at least one case, set off grenades, and killed several Marines. We were out of touch with the battalion.

About 9 p.m., we reestablished communications. The battalion came over the air, frantic at our loss of communications with them. They told us the NVA were out looking for us. Apparently, division intelligence had monitored an

NVA transmission. Division told the battalion to alert us that the Ninety-First Sapper Battalion was looking for us. When they hadn't heard from us at our scheduled time to check in, they feared the worst.

That tidbit of information didn't do much for my night's sleep, especially since the guy bringing up the rear had reported that someone had been watching us. We also made quite a bit of noise that night, wrestling with some little animals over a C-Rat can that one of my men had not properly put away. I had a makeshift team made up from various platoons. Teams from my platoon would have crushed the can and put it in their pack to bring back. I didn't allow any smoking either. Tobacco smells, and I was determined not get killed because of someone else's habit or sloppiness.

About 5 a.m., I heard whispering and the breaking of brush. I had everyone quietly slip on his gear. We moved out of our harbor site and on to a ridge next to it. I set up a quick perimeter and had everyone finish putting camouflage on his face. We no sooner sat down than there were all sorts of noises and smashing of underbrush from just the other side of our harbor site. It sounded like the whole North Vietnamese Army was there and coming in our direction!

We were in a tough spot. The enemy was on one side of us and behind us was a ridge. There was no foliage between the top of the ridge and us. We could not move without being seen.

My hand shook as I called for an AO. An OV-10 came on station right way. Because the division had intercepted those enemy transmissions and expected trouble, they had him literally sitting in his aircraft, awaiting our call.

We could hear his engine before we were able to spot the aircraft. He came up on the net.

"Veal Stew (our call sign), this is Cloudburst (his call sign). Over,"

I whispered into the radio handset, "Cloudburst, this is Veal Stew. I can see you. We are at your two o'clock. We have marked our position with our air panels. Over."

"Veal Stew, I have you spotted. Over."

"Cloudburst, the enemy is about seventy-five meters to our north. Can you make some dummy gun runs to get their heads down while we scramble up and over the ridge? Over."

"Roger that, Veal Stew."

He zoomed in at virtually tree-top level. We used the sound of his engine to cover our noise as we beat a hasty retreat up and over the ridge, disappearing into the thick jungle on the other side.

"Cloudburst, this is Veal Stew. We are clear."

"Roger, Veal Stew."

The AO circled the area. He began making passes, firing his rockets and machine guns. He did an excellent job of thoroughly shooting up the area.

We put some distance from our former position then hid out the rest of the day. Just before dark, we moved up toward the mountaintop again and harbored until about 1 a.m. At 1 a.m. with air support alerted in case we ran into trouble, we moved to the top of the mountain to secure the LZ for the infantry. We arrived about 3 a.m., checked the

LZ for the enemy and for booby traps, then settled down to wait for the 3rd Battalion, 7th Marines to arrive.

It was tense. There only were seven of us, and the enemy had been following us. They knew where we were. Finally, a few hours after dawn, CH46s arrived carrying the infantry. Using hand signals, I guided the first of the choppers into the LZ. As soon as the first group got off the bird, I briefed their lieutenant, and we got on his bird and left. I was glad it was over. It is one thing to know the enemy was around, and quite another to know that they are looking specifically for you.

When we arrived at the LZ where the infantry were being staged, we were treated a little like celebrities. Marines surrounded team members, asking questions, and taking pictures. Apparently, the word of our hide and seek with the enemy had gotten out. I think most of them thought it inconceivable that anyone would volunteer to be dropped into enemy infested territory with just six or seven other Marines. I am sure they questioned our sanity, no doubt with good reason.

May 27, 1970

I heard the most crushing news today: The colonel isn't leaving until August 10. He is going on R & R tomorrow, so at least I won't have to go to the breakfast club with him. I dreaded the thought of it! He is going to Australia. He will probably set relations back years. Mike Hodgins is on patrol right now. They tried to put him in yesterday, but the enemy was waiting in the LZ. I guess it was a pretty exciting few minutes.

May 30, 1970

Things have been interesting. A Marine in my old platoon wrote a letter to his girlfriend, saying he had saved another guy's life in an ambush, was wounded while doing it, and was missing in action. He had one of his buddies sign the letter and send it. A couple of letters from the girlfriend came to the company office, pleading for information about the MIA (missing in action) boyfriend. The girlfriend claimed they were going to get married when he got home. The boyfriend said he knew nothing about it. However, his buddy didn't support him. Apparently, the boyfriend also told his girlfriend that his father was KIA in Vietnam and his mother was in Paris. All not true. That Marine might want to sign up for another tour. Going home for him might be more dangerous than staying.

June 2, 1970

Yesterday was a bad day for Recon. A team was getting emergency extracted, and either someone on the team or the helicopter hit a booby trap. The result was two dead, one from Recon, and a couple hurt pretty badly. The helicopter was completely destroyed. Last night, there was a racial incident in one of the companies. One guy got his rifle and cut loose on three others. Fortunately, none of them was hurt too badly. Of course, with an M16 you don't have to be hit too badly for it to do a job. The colonel is on R & R. He will blow his stack when he gets back.

June 6, 1970

Yesterday and last night were exciting, too exciting with me as the officer of the day. First, one of the trash bins caught on fire, and the fire department was called. Actually, the trash was just smoldering. However, we found three boxes of .45 caliber ammunition in there. That would have made a nice explosion! That night, there was a fight at the enlisted USO show. The company commander of the guy who got beat up came to me and wanted some prompt action in finding the culprit. Like an idiot, I took the guy back to the outdoor theater to identify his attacker. Well, it turned out that the fight started over some racial remarks the white kid (the one who got beat up) made. When I paraded the white kid in front of the crowd to identify the guy who beat him up, it nearly started a riot! It really had me worried. There were about fifteen to twenty black Marines wandering around the battalion area. Fortunately, they decided to talk to the sergeant major and blow off steam that way. Then someone from S3 called to say they heard that a Marine locked and loaded his M16 and walked into Echo Company area. That caused a panic. It turned out to be the sentry. When I got relieved today, the major really chewed me out for referring to the fight incident as a near-race riot. Even the mention of a race riot gets the division really upset. In some Army units, the relationship between races is terrible, even deadly.

I went to sick bay this morning to see about having a little tumor in my back removed. The medical staff's eyes lit up at the prospect of some surgery! Their eyes, I might add, were bleary from last night's hangover. They brushed off the operating table (it had dirt from someone else's boots), whipped out the needle and scalpel, and told me to take off my shirt and lie down! The doctor jokingly assured me that he wasn't sure he would get the tumor, but he could guarantee a scar. At that point, I reconsidered the whole affair, grabbed my cover (hat), and made a quick exit.

Booby Trap

June 8, 1970

We hit a booby trap. We were inserted about 10 a.m. and were out by 4 p.m. We landed on an old fire support base on Charlie Ridge. We walked off the fire support base, keeping to the high ground. We had two Korean Marines with us who didn't speak English. Every time we sat down, they seemed to go to sleep. That didn't inspire a lot of confidence, especially as they were on point.

We saw an abundance of signs that US infantry had occupied the area. There were numerous foxholes. All vegetation had been removed to create firing lanes and eliminate cover for the enemy. We had nothing to conceal our movement. *Bam*! An explosion! Everyone hit the deck! It took a minute to work out what had happened. Sgt. Crawford, who was walking behind my radioman, stepped on a booby trap.

The corpsman reacted immediately. He rushed to Sgt. Crawford's side and began working on his wound. The corpsman reacted instinctively, giving no thought that he might step on hidden mine. That is one example of why Marines value and protect their corpsmen. I told everyone else to stay put. I didn't want anyone else stepping on a booby trap. I got back to the wounded Marine, trying to reassure him as the corpsman worked on him. Most of his foot was missing. I set up security and called in a medevac.

We waited anxiously, listening for the helicopter, knowing that the explosion had exposed our presence. Our corpsman stanched the bleeding, wrapped Sgt. Crawford's wound, and injected him with a syrette of morphine. There was little else he could do. Finally, the helicopter arrived. I directed it to our position. There was no place for the helicopter to land, so it lowered the jungle penetrator as it hovered over us. We situated Sgt. Crawford securely on the penetrator. He was slowly lifted out of the jungle and into the hovering helicopter. As soon he was aboard, the helicopter swept off for First Med.

I had a real scare getting out of Charlie Ridge. The medevac with all its noise and activity thoroughly compromised our patrol, so we moved back to the abandoned fire support base to await extraction. We had a long tense wait. Charlie Ridge was a notoriously bad area. It was called Charlie Ridge because invariably any US units who went in there made contact with Charlie (a nickname for the NVA/VC). There were a lot of Charlies on Charlie Ridge!

Finally, our extract helicopter arrived. With a huge sigh of relief and a dubious sense of security, we boarded. With us aboard, the helicopter swooped down from the ridge, quickly losing altitude. My anxiety level peaked. We were in an area where the NVA reputedly had .51 caliber machine guns. Those machine guns had no trouble shooting helicopters right out of the air. Looking out the window, I saw smoke streaming from the chopper. I definitely had a moment of panic. I thought the engine had gone, and we were headed straight into the ground. There was nothing but trees and NVA below! I started breathing again when the helicopter began gaining altitude, and the enemy hadn't started shooting. It turned out that we had to pick up another team, and the pilot was lightening the load by releasing fuel and swooping down to gain speed before climbing over the mountains. Whew!

I visited Sgt. Crawford in the hospital before he was flown out of the country. He had little to say. I am sure he was pretty doped up on pain meds. His foot was wrapped up, so it was hard to tell the extent of the damage, and I didn't want to ask him.

June 10, 1970

I thought there might be some fireworks when the colonel got back from R & R, and I was right. The day after he returned, he fired a lieutenant from Alpha Company.

From the time he was fired, it took a record of nine minutes to have the lieutenant's orders cut and for him to be on his way out of the battalion. The colonel has fired so many people that S1 (personnel) is getting really good at getting orders cut. The officers the colonel fires all get assigned elsewhere. They just lose the right to be in our unit. In this battalion, we are not only making the lion's share of the contact with the enemy in the division, but when in the rear, we walk on eggs for fear of getting fired. We also are taking our share of the casualties. I have to say, though, I am glad I got into Recon, and I am proud to be a member. The colonel doesn't allow any of his officers to get slack. It is hard not to feel like a member of a very select group.

June 13, 1979

Our insert was unremarkable, but as always, we are wet. If it is not raining, we are covered in sweat. After a few days, we all smell of mildew. Our uniforms are sodden. The jungle itself emits the pungent odor of decay. We communicate in whispers and hand signals. Having covered part of our haven, we set a perimeter and quietly took a rest break. I noticed the eyes of the man next to me fix on something in the jungle. His hand edged toward the trigger of his rifle. The hair on my head stood up. I began to bring my rifle around when a piercing shriek rent the jungle followed by crashing bushes. A rock ape walked up, not noticing us. The Marine next to me saw him and began preparing for the worst. When the rock ape spotted us, he took off with enough noise to wake the dead. It certainly took a few years off my life.

Other than that, the highlight of the patrol was the leeches. We cover all our skin, except our faces where we use a combination of bug repellent and camouflage paint, and bind our pants around our boot tops to keep the leeches out. Even so, we frequently find a leech attached to some part of our body. When we sat down, we could see the leeches coming, almost like someone sounded a bugle. We have excellent bug repellent that, when squirted on a leech, fried them. Frying leeches is a break time entertainment.

June 24, 1970

Things are busy. The chief, Lieutenant Pino, is going home tomorrow. Lt. Dyer, who took my platoon, is on the Sanctuary having a growth removed. Also, one of our patrol leaders jumped from a helicopter into his LZ and messed up his knee. Another patrol leader had a bad ulcer attack. The result is two platoons without platoon commanders, and two teams without team leaders. I get Lt. Dyer's patrol tomorrow.

June 28, 1970

I got out of the bush a day early because one of my team members came down with malaria. We had to medevac him. The whole team was taken out because the medevac compromised our position. When I got back, I found I had received my orders: Twentynine Palms, of all places! The one place in the whole USA that I didn't want to go! It is in the middle of the Mojave Desert.

I visited John Graff in the hospital today. He was one of the original six from my basic school company who came directly to Vietnam. He was with the 1st Marines and was out checking lines at night. One of his men shot him in the stomach and leg, thinking he was the enemy. He has been operated on and is very weak, but he will be okay. Jim House, Fitz, and I have all been to see him at various times. It is about all he can do to squeeze our hand and smile. They keep him pretty heavily doped up.

June 30, 1970

The colonel was a little drunk last night at the club. He stopped me going out the door, and told me that I "was a good, steady, and reliable lieutenant" and that I had my "head and ass wired together," that I didn't have to worry, I would be spending the rest of my tour right here in Recon. I guess that was a compliment. He said I wouldn't be going, meaning being fired from my post in the battalion.

July 2, 1970

I have been spending my days hassling with minor problems that come up in the company and writing end of tour awards. Two teams from my old platoon went out today, and I felt really guilty about not going. They asked me if I were going with them. That made the guilt even worse. This is the first time I haven't gone out or been out when they went to the bush.

July 3, 1970

Recon will stand down August 23 and be on the boat September 6. We are going home. The commandant of the Marine Corps is touring Vietnam this month, so we are on a big beautification jag in the battalion area.

9

Getting Short

July 13, 1970

My team was designated to provide security for the commandant's visit to the OP. Walking off the OP following a trail running along an adjacent ridge, we turned a corner and walked straight into an enemy bunker. It was unoccupied. Once again, our luck held! Had it been occupied, we would have been dead meat. There was no way we could have seen it before we walked up on it. On a ridge, with no foliage to cover us, there was nowhere to walk but on the trail. We harbored up a short distance from the OP so we would be in a position to give plenty of warning if the enemy chose to attack the OP during the commandant's visit.

Another team led by Lt. Dyer was inserted on the other side of our OP to provide early warning. They got into contact that night, and the light show was spectacular. Artillery was firing, and Spooky came on station. Spooky was a C130 aircraft loaded with Gatling guns and flares.

Flares were dropped at intervals. Spooky rained fire around the team's position. With its tracer rounds, it looked like a huge fire hose coming from the aircraft. They are able to put a round every foot of an area the size of a football field. We listened on the radio and watched the action. Finally, the team was extracted. We remained spectators.

July 17, 1970

I just came off patrol today and had some very sad news. One of the lieutenants in the S3 broke his back practicing a repelling exhibition for the commandant's visit. He will be paralyzed from the waist down, if he lives. He later died. Another Marine also was killed in the same accident. The lieutenant, Pete Gray, was one of the most genuinely nice people I know. Apparently, they repelled into Recon's LZ, but they were not able to disentangle themselves from the rope before the helicopter pulled off, dragging the two Marines through the wire and a strand of trees.

What an incredible waste of life! Any life lost here is a waste, but this seemed particularly egregious. They were practicing to put on a dog and pony show for the commandant, not anything vital to carrying out a reconnaissance mission. It highlights the randomness of death. What they were doing was not inherently dangerous. Things just went wrong.

Mike Hodgins completely rebuilt the OP for the commandant's visit. All new sandbags for the bunkers, and the battalion issued new utilities for his men, new helmet covers, the works. Mike was in his glory when the commandant visited. He did a very good job too.

July 27, 1970

We had a team shot out today. No casualties, but some of the team came back with bullet holes in their clothing. Their corpsman (it was his first patrol) refused to go back. Hodgins gave him one of the most stirring patriotic pep talks I have ever heard. I was fired up and ready to go myself! However, the corpsman was having none of it. He said not only no, but *hell* no! No way was he going out there again. It was way too dangerous! We threw him out of the company. What a bum. Most of our corpsmen are truly great. Anyone can be scared, but most can or at least try to control their fear.

July 28, 1970

I was the insert officer today as we tried to insert the team that got shot out yesterday. I was peering out of the back of the helicopter as it spiraled down into the zone. We started taking heavy fire. Everyone opened up out the windows and rear of the helicopter. They were yelling and spraying the LZ with rifle fire. Shell casing were popping all over the floor of the helicopter, adding to the din created by the engine, rifle fire, and yelling. The pilots pulled the helicopter up in an emergency assent.

When I suggested an alternate LZ, the pilots vetoed it and took us back to our helipad where they could inspect their helicopter for bullet holes. They weren't interested in going back for another try. The team wasn't either.

July 31, 1970

I got stuck being the battalion watch officer tonight. It was the end of a very hectic day. The battalion commander, two generals, and I visited the OP. We acquitted ourselves very honorably. Tomorrow, I am pay officer, and the colonel inspects the company area.

August 1, 1970

The colonel inspected our area, and we slid by somehow. He checked the officers' hooch for the first time, and for the first time, I hadn't cleaned the damn thing. But we lucked out! He was feeling benevolent. As we were leaving the company area, the colonel turned to me and said, "Well, Curry, you are one of the last of the veterans." Coming from the colonel that made my head swim and my chest swell with pride. Despite it all, the colonel's opinion meant something to all of us.

August 7, 1970

I got my flight date today. Jim House goes home the twelfth, Mike Hodgins the thirteenth, and I go the fourteenth. We all wanted to go home together since we came together. We will leave Vietnam and stopover in Okinawa for anywhere from seven to fourteen days.

The colonel's going-away party was a smashing success, literally. Apparently, it was so smashing that the division is investigating it. I was the battalion watch officer, so I missed it.

August 11, 1970

One of the men on duty in the office came running into my hooch yelling about a sentry dog that had taken over the company office. As it turned out, the dog just walked into the office, and both men there leaped for the desktops. One of them was sort of cornered on top of the first sergeant's desk. The other slipped out the door to get me. The dog, in the meantime, took up residence under the clerk's desk. Hodgins came down with me. He called the 3rd MPs to get a dog handler. I, believing discretion the better part of valor when it came to sentry dogs, remained in the back room close to the door.

After contacting the MPs and the interior guard, Mike and I went back to bed, leaving instructions with the duty to leave the dog alone and keep him in the office until the handlers arrived. Unfortunately, as soon as the dog moved, the duty jumped for the desktop again instead of closing the door. The guard spent the next three hours looking around the area trying to find the dog. It is hard to sleep. I am excited about going home.

If you are one of the lucky ones, you leave Vietnam after your twelve- or thirteen-month tour like you entered. I reported to the Da Nang Airport to be manifested on a flight to Okinawa. I stayed overnight and flew out the next day. I spent several days at Camp Hanson in Okinawa, waiting to be manifested on a flight to the United States. Red, my wife, and my parents met me at the airport. It was great to be back!

I fought my war as a Marine Corps infantry officer in a combat unit at the point of the spear. It was exactly where I chose to be. I was lucky. I came home in one piece. Fifty-eight thousand American servicemen and women were not so lucky. Vietnam was not a popular war, and many in the public arena took that out on those of us who went. I have an affinity for the military and a real sense of satisfaction in having served. I hold those who actually put his or her life on the line for our country in high esteem. I have absolutely no regard for those hawks that are quite comfortable letting someone else serve, take the risks, and do the fighting.

I left the Marine Corps. I seriously thought of making it a career. But then I didn't. It remains a high point in my life in which I take a great pride! Like most current and former Marines, I might add. Becoming a member of the United States Marine Corps is difficult. It requires individuals to summon resources they may not have known they possessed. Consequently, the Marine Corps is a fraternity for life. The words *Semper fidelis* (always faithful) have real meaning.

At any rate, what to do next, that was the big question.

10

Peace Corps Jamaica

Training

May 1972

"Ask not what your country can do for you. Ask what you can do for your country."

Those words of John F. Kennedy reverberated in my mind after leaving the Marine Corps and in the year it took to obtain my teacher's credential. Red worked in a Montessori school. We still felt the need to serve and to do our part in helping others. Consequently, we applied for the Peace Corps. We also wanted to experience the adventure of living in another country and learning about another culture, not something a tourist could do. We were offered either Korea or Jamaica. We chose Jamaica.

In July 1972, Red and I entered Peace Corps training. First we went to Washington, D.C. for an introduction to the Peace Corps. From there, we flew into Kingston, Jamaica. Peace Corps and the Peace Corps mission were iconic. It was exciting to actually become part it. As usual, I came down with a major anxiety-driven headache. Red adjusted to it all beautifully.

Once in Kingston, we were billeted in an old great house, something right out of the colonial era, located next to where the governor general lived in his official residence, another great house. The great houses sat amidst some lush tropical foliage. I don't think there was any air-conditioning. The rather elegant rooms were situated to allow air to flow through them. There were lots of lizards on the walls and giant moths, which the Jamaicans referred to as rat bats. They flew around the rooms and added to the exotic nature of what we were experiencing. During meals, everyone would meet in the dining room. The dining room was filled with small tables covered with white tablecloths. Very proper older folks were sitting at each table, talking in hushed tones. It all looked very British. I fully expected Colonel Mustard with his sweeping walrus mustache to stand up, give a loud harrumph to gain attention, and propose a toast to the Queen. It didn't happen, but we didn't exactly fit into the scene. We were dressed very casually. At that time, affluent Jamaicans dressed rather formally.

Any time we went anywhere, we had to hitchhike or take a bus or a minivan. That certainly added to the experience. We would stand at a bus stop in Kingston on a busy, dusty street with a crowd of Jamaicans, waiting for what we hoped would be the right bus. The bus would arrive, and the waiting crowd would all rush to board it at once. The whole British concept of queuing up for, well, anything, was lost. The buses were all overcrowded, standing room only, and really stinky as no one seemed to have gotten too close to a shower. It was very, very hot, which did nothing to reduce the aroma. In all fairness, many of the poor simply didn't have bathing facilities available to them.

The training was interesting. It included courses on culture, history, and even some language since the Jamaicans speak patois that, when they got going, I could never understand. Part of our training took us out to spend a weekend with a Jamaican family. We hitchhiked to the North Coast where we stayed with a Jamaican family who lived in St. Ann's Bay. I don't remember too much about that except the breakfast. We had really red-looking weenies, boiled bananas, and ackee, sitting on our plates. Ackee, the national fruit, looks something like scrambled eggs when it cooked. Unripe ackee is poisonous. We didn't know what to make of the breakfast. Boiled bananas have a very suspicious anatomical appearance. However, not wanting to insult our hosts, or Freud, we had red weenies and boiled bananas for breakfast. It turned out it was not an uncommon meal. Ackee frequently is served with saltfish.

After returning to Kingston and a few more classes, we were assigned to our parishes. Our parish was St. Elizabeth on the other end of the island from Kingston. We went looking for a house in the small town of Black River. My job was to organize guidance programs in the parish, and Red was assigned to be part of a reading program operated by one of the bauxite companies.

We caught the number six bus to Spanish Town on the outskirts of Kingston, and from there, we took another bus that went to Black River. The bus was packed, and, of course, there was no air-conditioning. It was an eight-hour bus ride.

The bus pulled up at the Mandeville market where some passengers disembarked, and others embarked with their purchases. Crowds of people were bustling about, bargaining and buying from the various vendors. It wasn't long before someone noticed us, two white faces, peering out the bus window at all of the noise and activity. It was unusual to see white faces on a public bus.

A crowd began to form under our window. Comments flew followed by pointing, lots of laughter, and capering. The crowd was thoroughly enjoying the specter of the two of us on the bus.

"Wa de du? Wa du dem?"

"We yu go? De tiicha."

"Me aks yu fi moni."

"Mi sari fi si we yu kom do un tu."

It was all patois. We didn't understand any of it. We were the focus of their entertainment. Red and I were feeling decidedly uncomfortable. We didn't like being the center of attention, and we had no way of knowing whether or not we should be concerned for our safety. After what seemed like an excruciatingly long time, the bus finally pulled off for Black River. We gave a sigh of relief.

Black River, a small old picturesque town situated on the coast, is the seat of St. Elizabeth Parish. There, the Black River flowed into the sea.

Along the main street were a few shops, a Chinese restaurant, a government house, and an old Anglican church with a small graveyard.

On Sundays despite the heat, you would see men dressed in their best dark suit and tie, and women, wearing long dresses and hats, walking to church. Contemporary informality and life's fast pace had yet to insinuate itself into their staid environment.

A hospital, which we visited, occupied a space along the road near the ocean. It was a small, one-story building, housing most of the patients in an open-air bay. There was no air-conditioning, but a gentle breeze off the ocean came through open windows and circulated through the room. Beds had gauzy curtains that could be pulled around them for some privacy. Nurses in white uniforms tended the patients. The hospital reminded me of something out of a World War II–era movie. Presumably, the most serious cases went to Kingston's major medical facilities, including a medical school.

Today, Black River is a tourist attraction. It looks nothing like it did when we arrived in 1972. In fact, that can be said for Jamaica as a whole.

We got off the bus and wandered through the town. We were there to find housing, but we didn't have a clue where to start looking. We ended up checking out three unoccupied cottages set along the beach about a mile from the town of Black River. The cottages were picturesque but seldom used. I am sure that had to do with the muddy water caused by the river and the no-see-ums, vicious little mosquito like critters that bite like crazy. According to the caretaker, lovers occasionally met in the cottages for afternoon trysts. The caretakers were an older couple, raising two of their grandchildren. They burned and sold charcoal to help make ends meet.

We asked about renting one of the cottages, telling the caretaker we only could afford about $50 a month. She contacted the owner, who agreed, figuring, I guess, that some money is better than no money at all. It was a nice little two-bedroom cottage with no air-conditioning. We burned coils in any room we were in to get rid of mosquitos and no-see-ums. The setting was great, very picturesque. The reality—no-see-ums, muddy water—not so much. However, we felt fortunate to have found a place to live.

After exploring the town, we returned to Kingston. We hitchhiked. We had, had enough of the bus. Besides, it was much quicker to hitchhike. We went from Black River to Kingston fairly frequently for meetings or to plan training for new volunteers. We hitchhiked. We always picked one of the newer, better model cars, preferably a Jaguar. They were more comfortable and, with luck, the drivers drove more cautiously than was common in Jamaica.

On our trip through Mandeville to Black River, I noticed a rugby pitch (field). While hitchhiking on a sub-sequent trip to the North Coast, we were picked up by an Irish couple, Jimmy and Barbara Smyth. They were teach-ers who lived in Mandeville. I asked them about the rugby pitch about the same time that Jimmy asked me if I played. It made my day! Playing rugby had been my passion since college. We hitchhiked to Mandeville every weekend to play. Someone on the team always put us up for the week-end, or gave us a ride if the game was out of town.

Getting started working in St. Elizabeth was a challenge. Red was supposed to teach reading in a bauxite company-sponsored program. The program shut down, and she ended up teaching remedial reading at the local elementary school, Black River Elementary.

We walked into the school and introduced ourselves to the principal, Mrs. Reynolds. Around us, students were reciting lessons in their various classrooms. It was a noisy, busy environment. The elementary school was an open-air facility, built in the shape of a U made out of cement blocks. The inside of the U was completely open. Each of a row of classrooms was divided from the next classroom by a portable blackboard. Much of the teaching was done by rote recitation so students in the back row had a much better chance of hearing the class behind them than their own. Many times, teachers took their classes outside to sit under a shade tree complete with resident goats to teach their lessons.

Wooden desks sat three students across at each desk. The government set the student-teacher ratio at fifty students to one teacher. Students all wore uniforms. Many had only one uniform, and when it got dirty, or on market days when they helped their mothers, they didn't attend school. Teacher-administered corporal punishment was the norm for inattentive or misbehaving students. Many teachers carried a strap, which they applied liberally when they felt inclined.

Mrs. Reynolds, a very distinguished-looking lady, welcomed us. She worked out a plan so Red could regularly teach a group of students. In addition to reading, Red ended up teaching some sex education classes. She got tired of boys giving her wolf whistles as she rode her bike back and forth to school and decided to provide some proper sex education instruction. I don't think it had much impact on the wolf whistles.

I was supposed to establish guidance programs in the parish schools. Since I had no transportation and buses were not really reliable, I confined my activities to Black River Elementary School and Black River Junior Secondary School. I wasn't sure what setting up a guidance program actually entailed. I set up some career days and cumulative record systems that I encouraged teachers to pursue. The teachers, like teachers everywhere, were more concerned with their everyday classroom issues than in establishing new programs.

Ultimately, I ended up teaching English and Jamaican history at the junior secondary school. Mr. Harris was the principal. That was an interesting experience. I taught English to a group of students who, when I asked a question, answered in patois that left me clueless. I have no doubt they thoroughly enjoyed the whole situation.

My Jamaican history class was even worse. I would stand at the portable blackboard, trying to talk over the noise of the band next door. The classes were separated by a sliding divider that would not completely close. I would talk, and the tuba would play. I would talk louder, and the drums would roll. I would talk faster between compositions. I handed out written notes. But I found I had a class of nonreaders. So I went back to talking faster between compositions.

At the time, the Jamaican educational system reflected the English model. Elementary school students were given the eleven-plus exam. That exam pretty much dictated their educational future. If they scored high enough, they went on to secondary school and then college or university. If they didn't get the requisite score, they went to the junior secondary school and that concluded their formal education.

Settling In

We have been here seventeen months, and we have adjusted well. We thoroughly enjoy our Jamaica experience. We are on Jamaican time, that is, late to almost everything except rugby games. That was an easy accommodation, but it is more difficult adjusting to the various and sundry shortages. In addition, someone always seems to be on strike.

Any time our power goes off, which it regularly does, or we can't get gas, or buy staples at the grocery store, it gets to be a challenge. When a local fire department struck, a house burned down. During the jail guards' go slow, three convicts escaped. And so it goes. For a while, the police and the Army (who can't strike) were shooting it out with each other. Fortunately, they have returned their attention to the criminals. Shortages also are common, and they cover the whole spectrum from canned milk, rice, flour, sugar, matches, cooking oil, tuna, and rum. Sugar! It is grown here! Rum! Now that hurts! What's a rum bar without rum! The reggae still blasts from roadside rum bars though! And you still can get Red Stripe beer.

Every weekend we go to the market to do our shopping for the following week. Red has certain ladies (called higglers) from whom she buys her produce, never everything from one lady, but a few things from each. Sunday through Thursday, the Black River market is deserted. The market is open air, consisting of a tin roof and supporting pillars. Early Friday morning it begins to awaken as the first higglers arrive with their goods. By late Friday afternoon, it is teeming with activity.

Saturday morning is bedlam. People dressed in their Sunday best talk, yell, joke, bargain, quarrel, and generally socialize with each other. It is so crowded that you can hardly move. Pigs and goats persistently nose about the garbage. Donkeys stand stoically, awaiting loading or unloading by their owners. Above the din can be heard, "Kisko. Kisko Pops," cried out by a boy, dispensing them from a box on his bicycle. Another man, selling snow cones from a cart is shouting, "Ice. Ice." A different vendor chimes in, "Cream. Cream," offering homemade ice cream. A man leans against a wall, housing the public toilet, urinating.

Each higgler sits regally surrounded by her wares: mangos, tomatoes, cucumbers, cabbage, yams, oranges, onions, potatoes, scallions, bananas, and watermelons. "Mistress. Mistress." "Buy from me, Mum." "Nice salad." "Yam. Yam for you today?" The higglers usually wear colorful full skirts that they allow to droop between their knees forming something of a counter on which they can conduct their business. They sport brightly colored plaid headscarves and keep their money tightly wrapped in a handkerchief held in their apron pocket.

In another part of the market is the meat section. Butchers stand in their stalls, wearing blood-spattered aprons, skillfully cutting meat with their machetes. Pig or cow carcasses line the aisle. Pig heads and feet or cow tails and skins are displayed under the stalls. The musty smelling area is dimly lighted with an odor of fresh meat. Outside, people can be seen milling about the gates with their purchases. All sorts of means are used to transport goods. In a basket atop a woman's head is the most common way; donkeys, bicycles, wheelbarrows, overcrowded taxis and busses are others.

After spending a year hitchhiking around the country with drivers whose driving habits continually made one feel that death was imminent, we bought a car. Trucks park in the middle of the road, on blind corners, without lights. Motorists pull out and stop in the middle of narrow streets whenever the spirit moves them to chat with friends for indefinite periods. Motorists regularly pass on blind corners. It is hair raising. We feel, though, that with our own car, we have at least a little more control over our destiny. We like to think of our car as a classic. Some less-reverent souls have had the audacity to refer to it as an old rattletrap. It is a 1958 right-hand drive MG Magnette. You drive on the left in Jamaica.

Being a shrewd judge of cars, we have only had to do some minor repairs such as the clutch, valves, rings, brakes, etc., since buying the car. Finding a good mechanic can be a real challenge. Ours literally works under a large shade tree. One of our friends took his car in for some work, and it has never run right since. He finally sold it out of sheer frustration. A lady wanted a minor job done on her car. When she returned to drive it away, she put it in first gear and reversed into the wall behind her. One gets very philosophical after a while.

Signs along the road advertise condoms in a government effort to get a handle on birth control and STDs. Originally, the condoms advertised were made in Japan. That had to be changed though. No self-respecting Jamaican male was going to admit to using a condom made in Japan! Reputedly, the government got around that by marking them all extra large.

Not too long ago, as a change from hitchhiking, we took the train to Montego Bay. It is a charming trip! The train is old and rickety as is the station. They are right out of the 1930s. The scenery was beautiful. Cane fields followed by thick foliage, then the steep, hilly Cockpit Country where bands of runaway slaves repeatedly defeated the British Army. All along the line, little houses perched precariously on the hillsides. One wonders why they don't come tumbling down during the rainy season. Always, people stop to watch the train pass. It is a highlight in their day. We even caught one man in a stream in the middle of his bath. For some very un-Jamaican reason, he covered his loins as we passed. Modesty does not seem to be a character trait of Jamaican men. Lack of public restrooms is never a hindrance. A preacher boarded soon after we left our station. He went from car to car, giving the same spiel. He would pass out hymn sheets and give a short sermon. He would then lead his flock, captive audience, in song as he took up donations. Heathens that we are, we remained aloof and declined to donate. He gave up on us early as truly unsalvageable.

The train was a great way to see the country!

Kingston

There isn't much to do in Black River for entertainment, so whenever we go to Kingston, we enjoy seeing a movie. There is nothing like a good spaghetti western. Not that the movies are good, but the audiences are fantastic! As the pace of the action heightens, the audience becomes increasingly excited and vocal. Each punch in a good movie land brawl is greeted with a deafening roar. It sounds like a football stadium at the climax of a close game. Tender love scenes are greeted with hoots of derision and/or ribald comments. During the movie *Jesus Christ Superstar*, Mary Magdalene was tendered all sorts of helpful suggestions when she sang, "I don't know how to love him."

There are several stories passed around by Peace Corps volunteers about how seriously some Jamaicans take their movies. One of these stories involves an extremely suspense-filled western. The audience was sitting attentively in one of the few Kingston movie theaters, and as the movie built toward a climax, tension gripped the spectators. They were on the edge of their seats. In the final showdown, the hero stood alone, unaware as the villain crept up from behind. Someone in the audience shouted, "Look out! Him behind yu!" Just then, the hero turned, spied the villain, and shot him. An admirer of the villain in the audience leaped from his seat bellowing, "Yu tel 'im!" and promptly punched the guy who shouted the warning.

We were sitting outside a little place in downtown Kingston, enjoying a Jamaican pate. A naked man came wandering down the busy street, carrying on a heated conversation with himself. People passed him by. No one seemed to take particular notice. He turned a corner and disappeared down a side street. Soon after, two police constables came hurrying down the street, turning down the same side street. We sat there munching our pates, observing it all with detached curiosity. How would the police handle this? Soon, the two constables returned to continue their business. A few minutes later, the naked man reappeared. This time he had a cardboard box tied with twine around his waist, covering the necessary parts. Problem solved! It was a sensible solution that wouldn't have happened in the US.

Our Black River cottage with our most prized "classic"
the MG Magnette sitting in front of it.

The town of Black River 1972

Black River Elementary School. The shade tree
often provided an outdoor classroom.

Inside Black River Elementary School. Note the
portable blackboards separating the classes.

The Black River Market. On market days it was packed with people.

Caretakers of the cottages where we lived. They are carrying a
tin of the charcoal they sold to supplement their income.

Haiti

Ever since I read Graham Green's novel *The Comedians*,
I had been intrigued with Haiti. Papa Doc and his secret
police, the *Tonton Macoute*, terrorized the country. But
Papa Doc was dead, and Baby Doc now ruled a country.
Haiti not only had an interesting and turbulent history but
also produced some unique artworks.

On a previous visit to Port-au-Prince, we stayed in
the Hotel Oloffson, the hotel that was the inspiration for

Graham Greene's hotel. I loved being immersed in this setting, and I looked forward to another opportunity to explore Haiti.

We arrived in Port-au-Prince with the intention of traveling cross-country to Cap-Haïtien and the famed Citadel of King Christophe. The following morning, we went to the bus depot bright and early to begin our trip to Cap-Haïtien, the historical capital. We were immediately engulfed by a mob of babbling bus drivers. We picked one who looked respectable, and Red conducted a short quiz on driving safety in Pidgin English.

The buses actually were big gaily decorated trucks modified to carry people. A crowd of vendors, carrying their goods on their head, milled around the buses, selling chicle (gum), soap, sunglasses, socks, crackers, hats, bread, drinking glasses, food, thermoses, you name it. Beggars wandered around, holding their hands up to the bus windows, fixing each passenger with a pitiful, pleading, accusing look. Many beggars in Haiti look truly pitiful with a range of ailments and every god-awful disease imaginable. By comparison, Jamaica is a very healthy and prosperous country. Jamaica certainly appears to be a happier country.

On the way out of town, we passed the town dump dotted with squatting men, women, and children, relieving themselves. The adjacent area was literally covered with little shacks made from assorted scraps. The roads, and I use the term recklessly, ranged from mostly unpaved to cobblestone. It was impossible to exceed 20 mph. The countryside was largely scrub brush. The small clusters of houses that we passed were made of mud with thatched roofs. Many children had distended bellies. Any problem of children outgrowing their clothes was neatly solved. They didn't wear any. Every so often we were stopped at security checkpoints manned by armed guards. Bathroom breaks entailed the truck stopping and women going to one side of the truck and men to the other side. After a ten-hour trip, we arrived in Cap-Haïtien tired, numb, and covered with dust. We signed in with the police and headed straight for our hotel, making sure to make plane reservations for the trip back.

The planned highlight of our trip was a visit to the citadel. In order to get there we had to walk or ride horses from a small town called Milot at the foot of the mountain. At Milot, we collected three horses, two carry boys apiece (one to push and one to pull the horse), and a guide. After a one-and-a-half-hour ride up a steep rocky trail, it was a relief to arrive!

The citadel is awe-inspiring. A massive stone fortress built by the first king of Haiti. Everything going into building the fortress had to be carried up the mountain, except the brick. It was never fully completed. In thirteen years of building, it cost 20,000 lives. King Christophe reputedly occasionally marched his troops over the edge of one of the high walls to demonstrate their discipline. After an all-too-brief visit, we started back to Milot. The ride down the mountain was hair raising. The carry boys rushed the horses pell-mell down a narrow trail strewn with rocks, the mountain on one side of the trail and a sheer drop off on the other. Red was frightened to death. I didn't feel any too secure either! We also discovered that we just didn't have callouses in the right places to be cowboys. At Milot, we found our taxi driver irate because we had taken longer than he had anticipated. Never mind that it was our money!

The trip to Haiti poignantly emphasized the lucky accident of our birth. One of the fundamental aspects of being a Peace Corps volunteer is the exposure to another culture. Haiti provided a stark reminder of how different our lives could have been. We, most Americans, are born and raised in a secure bubble where food, shelter, and freedom are not issues. My Peace Corps experience helped me grow as person much less likely to take for granted the life I had in the United States and to feel a deep compassion for those not as fortunate.

Red has been struggling with a diet off and on since we arrived in Jamaica. What Jamaicans eat and what we eat is loaded with starch. I get a lot of exercise, so I don't have too much to worry about. I have played at least one rugby game every weekend from the beginning of September until last weekend, the end of the season. It has been a good year for our rugby team. The team won league play and several tournaments. In addition, I was selected to play for the national team in a couple of international matches. I had a great trip to the Bahamas for one of our games as well as to Martinique for the Caribbean Rugby Championship. In another game, we beat a very good Argentinian side with a last minute drop goal. They were so upset at losing a game they dominated, they skipped the traditional after game party, refused to shake hands, loaded onto their busses, and left in a huff. It was always an honor as an American to be selected to play for Jamaica, a team dominated by some very good British players who had played the game their whole lives.

I also stay in shape by running down the road on which we live. Every evening as I run down the road, I pass the same lady, returning from the market, bushel on her head. Every evening I say hello in my best Peace Corps manner as I pass. Invariably, her response is "Pork!" Pork is a very unflattering Jamaican term for white people. That is the extent of our conversation and has become something of a ritual. I actually look forward to seeing her on the road so I can give her a cheery hello, and she with her terse reply, "Pork!" It is pithy, if nothing else. Your Peace Corps in action!

Red and I have been offered jobs teaching at an American school in Mandeville, Jamaica. The salary is better than I could get at home. And a big three-bedroom, two-bathroom house is provided in addition to a paid trip home each year. The company I would be working for is called International Schools Services. It offers an opportunity to be placed in schools throughout the world. It is a good deal, especially in view of the employment picture at home. If we were to come home, though, I probably wouldn't stay in teaching.

Jamaica is its same inimitable self. The government has decided that crime has just gotten too out of hand. It has too! They prosecute anyone caught with an illegal firearm. They have set up this ominous-looking building in Kingston, painted bright red, and called it gun court. It has gun towers and is surrounded by barbed wire. It holds those accused of gun crimes. Unfortunately, they only have sentenced one person. Another anticrime measure is to censor all shooting scenes from movies. That is, all scenes where the bad guy shoots the good guy are cut out. If the good guy is shooting the bad guy, it is sometimes left in. If the good guy is shooting himself, it is definitely cut out. As you can guess, this censorship often makes it a real challenge to follow the plot of the movie. It is best to go to movies in groups. In that way, each can contribute his opinion of what has taken place in the film. If this method doesn't always lead to an accurate assessment of the action, it at least lends variety.

Incidentally, gas is $1.20 a gallon here. The stations open at 8 a.m. and have stopped serving gas by 11 a.m. They close Saturday and Sunday, and there is always a line. Of course, at the end of the month, there usually isn't any gas, so one walks until the tanker arrives. The cost of living in Jamaica has doubled and tripled since we first came. I am wondering how and when this worldwide inflationary spiral is going to end!

On my way to Kingston for a trial selection match for the Jamaican National Rugby Team, I saw a man, looking very unsteady on his bike in front of my car. I slowed, and as I passed him, he weaved out and hit my car. I immediately pulled over to see if he was hurt. He wasn't hurt. He was drunk as a coot. Still, I wanted to take him to the local hospital and make sure he was okay. He objected, pulled out his knife, and came after me. It turned into a scene from a Charlie Chaplin movie. Keeping my distance, I jumped over a low rock wall bordering the house next to the road. He jumped over after me, and I jumped back to the other side. All the while, I tried to talk him down. We went round and round until the lady of the house, thoroughly disgusted, came out and told him to put his knife away and get in the car. He did. Women carry a lot of authority in Jamaica. In many respects, it is a matriarchal society.

We got to the hospital. I immediately informed the Red Stripe policemen on duty about the knife. They grabbed the inebriated cyclist, hauled him into the next room, and, judging from the noise, gave him a good pummeling. Relieved to be out of what could have been a dangerous situation, I wasted no time exiting the hospital and getting on the road to Kingston for the trial matches.

Malcolm Jardine, Mike Curry, Martin Brinn rehydrating after a win.

The Mandeville Rugby Team. We had some very good rugby players.

The Jabaas, Jamaican National Team. This was one
of the stronger Jamaica teams we fielded.

11

Mandeville

We were in a company home with a relatively small backyard a cow had somehow wandered into. I went out to remove the cow, grabbing the rope she was dragging. She took offense to this for some reason and pursued me more ardently than I had anticipated. Red heard my shouts for assistance. She found me frantically hot footing it around the yard one step ahead of the cow. The situation was saved when Red, recovering from spasms of near-hysterical laughter, picked up a stick and firmly directed the cow out the gate. I don't know why she found it so funny! The matador in me was envisioning being pierced by a horn in a very uncomfortable spot!

I started work at Belair School where, walking into the faculty room, I met a truly remarkable group of people. The faculty included at least one Welsh nationalist, a Canadian Olympic swimmer, a Brit who drove a landing craft onto the beaches on D-Day, an American married to a Russian woman, who was twice wounded in the Battle of the Bulge, a couple who had been evacuated from

Bangladesh, a Jamaican returned from living in the US so she could raise her children in Jamaica, and an American hippy who marched to the sound of his own drum. They had lived and worked all over the world! Just being around them was energizing. I loved the erudite conversations in the faculty room. Sipping our tea or coffee, we would have spirited discussions that took on and solved all of the world's problems. If the world had only listened! But, alas, our influence didn't extend beyond the faculty room.

After we left the Peace Corps, we signed contracts with International School Services to teach at Belair School in Mandeville. The school served the children of American bauxite workers and prepared British and Jamaican students for university or college. The bauxite companies fund the school and hire International School Services to staff it. It is a K–12 school with an international staff. I taught American history and English to the American students. British teachers prepared British/Jamaican students for their Ordinary and Advanced Level exams in the British system.

Mandeville was a desirable place to live. It is located in the mountains with a mild climate and an abundance of verdant foliage. It was not heavily populated, but it had a large market, various stores, schools, medical facilities, and a few restaurants. It was known as little England partly because low rock walls bordered many of the properties. As important to me, it had an excellent rugby pitch! Easily the best I ever played on.

In addition to a good job with terrific kids, a nice company house, a full-time live-in maid, and great friends, we have a daughter! She was born July 9, 1975 in Mandeville's hospital. I was in the room for the birth; totally useless, I might add. It wasn't like the movies. It was really messy. One look at Rachel covered in blood and whatever else, and I thought, *Geez, she looks just like my Uncle Keith; big, over-weight Uncle Keith. We'll have to educate her for sure.* Well, she was a beautiful little girl, of course. I was just a little overwhelmed from the whole birth trauma. If I had been the one enduring childbirth, we would have been a one-child family! Fortunately, Red did just fine. We named our daughter Rachel. It seemed a good strong Biblical name.

Rachel is the center of our life. As any parent knows, there is really no choice in the matter. Fortunately, we could not possibly have a better baby. She sleeps through every night, thoughtfully sleeping in on weekends, and is generally a happy little soul, except when tired or hungry (takes after her mother). She is very alert. As the Jamaicans say, "sensible" (taking after her father, no doubt), grabbing at things, putting everything into her mouth, and sitting up with a wee bit of help. Right now, she is doing the Mexican hat dance in her Jolly Jumper. While thoroughly enjoying our baby, we have reconsidered rushing out another as originally planned!

Unfortunately, we had to cancel our trip to Mexico City this Christmas. I severely injured my back doing assorted stupid things and am just now recovering from looking like Quasimodo.

Mexico wasn't the only disappointment due to my back. I was picked as part of the national squad to represent Jamaica in the Caribbean Rugby Championships in

Barbados, and I had to cry off. Jamaica ended up winning the championship. Captaining the Mandeville team from the sidelines has made me one of the most vocal, if not effective, captains.

Since we had to miss Mexico City, we spent a week in a cottage at Treasure Beach, about thirty miles from here. The weather was gorgeous, the water crystal clear, and the snorkeling fantastic. It is like swimming in a big aquarium. I would have enjoyed it more if scenes from *Jaws* hadn't kept flashing through my mind. I tried to console myself with the thought that the friend I was with looked much tastier than I did!

We have decided to invest the money we saved by not going to Mexico City in our 1958 MG Magnette. We have had it reupholstered, but we need to do a little body-work. Red was involved in an unfortunate incident. She was backing out of a parking place when an impertinent cement post jumped out from nowhere and smashed her right in the driver's door. Red immediately leaped out of the car to give the offending post a thorough tongue lash-ing. Finding the post unmoved by her tirade, she turned on two bystanders and reduced them to shriveled and quak-ing shadows of their former selves for being in the gen-eral vicinity. When she finally stormed into the house, still railing at the perfidy of that cement post, I was prudent enough not to mention that I had not recently run across many jumping posts, at least not of the cement variety.

We hope to stay here for the next year or two. We are very happy with our jobs. The conditions are good, and the students are great. All in all, it is a very pleasant place to live. Unfortunately, we may not have the choice. The economy has already forced one bauxite plant to close, and the others are cutting back sharply. The Jamaican government is replacing expatriates with Jamaicans, greatly reducing the American presence. Our jobs depend on bauxite funding for the education of American kids. The government also is turning increasingly to the left and aligning itself with the third world, specifically the Cubans. Many Jamaicans worry that the country may be flirting too much with communism. They are finding ways to get their money and themselves out of Jamaica. Next year is an election year, so things could get interesting. Quite a bit of politically inspired violence occurs during elections.

Politics

We still are in Jamaica, and life here is as interesting as ever. The national elections, which have caused considerable trauma among the populous, have just finished. The word was love, according to the People's National Party (PNP), which ran on that platform. However, insults, fists, brickbats, and bullets contributed to the campaign. With the elections drawing nearer, many people became panicky, feeling that blood was going to flow in the gutters. The Americans at Alpart, a large bauxite company, were flown out of the country, and the US Embassy started making contingency plans for evacuating all expatriates. All the flights out of the country were booked up. As things turned out, the elections were very quiet.

While the campaigning lasted, rhetoric flew thick and fast. The rabble rousing at rallies was sometimes incredible. The Jamaica Labour Party (JLP) blamed every conceivable ill on the PNP, including, at one point, a frigid wife. Now that is hitting below the belt, so to speak!

The PNP rally in Mandeville was a superb show of demagoguery. Prime Minister Manley had the crowd in the palm of his hand. He kept referring to Seaga, the opposition leader (spelled CIAga in PNP propaganda), as Rat Bat because he wears dark glasses. By the end of the rally, Manley had the crowd chanting, "Rat Bat lie. Rat Bat lie." How can American politics hope to compete with "Rat Bat lie" for sheer entertainment? Pretty catchy too! Compare it with "We want Carter." Rather bland! (Obviously, things have changed dramatically in American politics.)

Although the campaign rhetoric may not strain the intelligence, the government can be pretty crafty. When it looked as though the police and the Army were going to get into one of their periodic grudge wars, the government ordered policemen to guard the Army camps and soldiers to guard the police stations. This may have been a rather ridiculous sight, but the subtle exchange of hostages cooled things right down.

Our daughter is growing like a weed. She careens around the house, getting into everything. Nothing is safe. As our housekeeper says, "She has tall fingers." The consensus is that she is the image of her father, so we have decided that a good education is our best bet.

Red and I are again involved in the rugby club pantomime, a silly musical based on a fairy tale with lots of inside political jokes. All the British seem to be able to sing, and a male always plays the part of the lead female. The pantomime is one of the year's highlights in Mandeville, that should tell you something about our metropolis, and what keeps the rugby club solvent. That and the bar, I might add. Last year, we were in the chorus. What else do you do with people who can't sing, dance, or act? This year, I have been upgraded to the part of the mayor. It is a very minor-speaking part, in addition to the chorus. Red still is relegated to the chorus, which annoys her no end. And, of course, I do not rub it in. I might add on my first appearance on stage, I completely forgot my lines. I stood in front of the audience dumbfounded, a highly embarrassing situation. Someone off stage had to whisper them to me. The next day, my students made sure to bring it up in class.

We have just finished a trip around the island with my folks. Everything imaginable went wrong with our car, and we fully expected to come home and find our house had been broken into, which would top everything off. Our fears were not realized, but our confidence in the watchman was short-lived. We found out he had locked himself into the bathroom of our maid's quarters every night and slept soundly!

In September 1977, Adam was born. The doctor who delivered him was in my rugby club. Fortunately, he was a much better doctor than he was a rugby player. Everything is pretty casual in Jamaica, so I was able to be in the delivery room for both Rachel and Adam. Though educational, it solidly affirmed my opinion that I would not want to be a woman! Having babies is a messy and painful affair even under the best of circumstances. Red and I were really happy to have two healthy children: a boy and a girl.

After six really wonderful and interesting years and with two Jamaicans in the family, we left Jamaica. I planned to get a master's degree in school administration at Western Carolina University and then travel the world as an administrator in various American schools. We thought this an excellent way to see the world. In addition, corporation-funded schools generally paid well. They certainly paid better than most schools in the US. However, things seldom work out as planned. One example of the unexpected: The school we had talked with the president of International School Services about was in Isfahan, Iran. The Iranian revolution occurred and precluded any possibility of that happening. However, we did go ahead and get our degrees.

Okay, an overseas school was out of the question. I needed a job and, with a PhD minor in middle school education, Birmingham City Schools had an opening. I still felt a need to serve, which is how I viewed education, as well as be employed. I took what turned out to be a very naive leap into an unknown situation.

12

Middle School

August 1981

If this were a movie, it would be R rated. It is a story filled with sex, violence, and moral dilemmas. But it is not a movie. It is the story of an inner city middle school set during a tumultuous time.

The principal, Jim Griffin, and I were standing in the school bus with parents sitting in seats their children had been assigned.

Jim was talking, "I want you all to look at the back of the seat in front of you and at the condition of the seat where you are sitting. This bus was new this year."

There was a general groan and exclamations about the written obscenities and the vandalism they were viewing. In some cases their child's initials were evident.

"That is where your child is assigned to sit," Jim continued.

From the parents, "How do you know it was my child?"

"My child wouldn't write that!"

"Prove it!"

"You're just trying to blame my child!"

"This is bullshit!"

Despite Jim telling the parents that only their children rode that bus and the seats were all assigned, no parent was willing to take responsibility, or allow his/her child to take responsibility. It was an all-too-common theme.

Somewhere along the line, my marriage with Red fractured. We had issues that we couldn't seem to work through. Fortunately, we remained friends and worked well together with our children as our priority.

We both were offered jobs with the Birmingham School System. Red had gotten her master's degree in media and was employed as a media specialist in an elementary school. With my newly printed PhD from the University of Alabama, I was hired as a middle school assistant principal. I had been offered other jobs, but any job away from Birmingham would have taken me away from my children, an unacceptable situation. I wanted to be an involved father even though I didn't make the grade as a husband.[3]

What follows reflects a sample of the many issues, problems, and events that occurred during the thirty-one years I spent as a principal in the Birmingham system. It was a very tumultuous time in Birmingham with bussing and the integration of some schools in addition to gangs, drugs, and weapons. Many of the problems reached down

---

[3] On a quiet Sunday morning on June 2, 2002, a drunk driver who left the scene of the accident killed Red. She was bike riding on a wide untraveled road. The asshole never took his foot off the gas. Ultimately, he was arrested and sent to prison.

into the middle and even elementary schools. I recounted a variety of incidents, some relatively trivial and some quite serious, to illustrate the wide range and number of things that came up over the years. Therefore, it is less a story than simply a retelling of events. It could get pretty crazy. Over time, the almost daily and unrelenting barrage of significant issues was wearing on body and soul. Sanity frequently was maintained by finding some humor in a situation. A sense of humor was a critical asset for middle school survival.

Birmingham is an inner city school system with the diversity of issues reflective of the inner city, other than disciplinary issues, that occur in the schools. Many students came to school from very chaotic and dysfunctional family situations. There seldom were two parents in the home. Frequently, drug and alcohol abuse touched students' lives. Money and resources were scarce. Few had positive role models to provide them a plan and encouragement to join the middle class. They had no vision for the future. I encouraged teachers to provide a vision for what their students could become. That vision was the first step in achieving long-term goals.

Jefferson Middle School (grades 6 through 8), as were all the middle schools in Birmingham, was created under a court-ordered desegregation decree. Jefferson was fed by two elementary schools. Madison Elementary School, a white, mostly middle or upper middle class community, and Adams Elementary, a mostly blue-collar white community. Black students were bussed from mostly lower income communities in order to fulfill the desegregation decree.

Principals from the feeder schools that had been K–8 schools, now to become K–5 schools, designated teachers to go to Jefferson. This situation created a tremendous resentment among both parents and teachers. White parents began moving out of the area. Within about a five-year period, the neighborhood around Jefferson went from white to black. At one point, every house in the community behind Jefferson had a for-sale sign up. The tension created by the changing demographics in the community was felt in the school.

Race was an issue in virtually everything, whether dealing with parents, teachers, or students. It was the prism through which everything else was viewed. This was true for both white and black parents. Of course, ultimately, the majority of white parents moved out of the Birmingham school district and into various suburban districts. The same story was being repeated nationally.

The school system administration tried to stay sensitive to race relation. For example, I received a call from our director requesting information on the grades of one of our social studies teachers. The director wanted to know the number and race of each student who got an F. A parent had complained that the teacher was failing only black students. As it turned out, the teacher was very ecumenical in delivering failing grades.

Assistant Principal

I was the assistant principal my first two years at Jefferson and principal the subsequent fifteen years. The following are some notable instances I jotted down on my calendar during my tenure at Jefferson. This definitely is not a comprehensive account of events. In addition, situations such as most of the everyday discipline are not recorded.

I spent a lot of time walking the halls during class changes supervising student movement. One morning, a sixth grader stopped me in the hall to have me look at a rash on her neck. She explained that her mother had told her that since I was a doctor, I should be able to diagnose her problem. I had to admit that although I did a lot of things, the rash was not in my area of expertise.

Sight unseen we had arranged for an assembly sponsored by the American Freedom Assembly. This guy showed up dressed in jungle boots and camouflaged uniform with a ranger patch on his shoulder. He talked right-wing politics, distorting history, calling Roosevelt a traitor for Yalta; Truman and MacArthur complicit in the red Chinese takeover of Korea; Vietnam; and Carter's fiasco in Iran. Among other topics, he said the new generation of kids were not measuring up to their responsibilities and not willing to die for their country; the Russians were taking over; and ended with a spiel about Jesus Christ his savior. In other words, he broke about every legal rule of politics and religion in public schools. I was horrified! I fully expected to get a call from the ACLU. However, no one else seemed to give it a second thought.

I received a call from a parent asking the attendance officer to check into his daughter's absences. He blamed his divorced wife for not getting her to school and allowing her to stay up late at night. Both mother and daughter would sleep late in the mornings. I talked to the attendance officer. I also was curious if and how mother held a job.

Wow! This could have really not turned out well. A seventh grader came to the office, said she was sick, and her mother was picking her up. Apparently, she then went outside presumably to wait for her mother. Her grandmother called after school and said her granddaughter was missing. We were informed that her father had custody of her and that her mother was in Michigan. No one had signed the girl out. The next day, the grandmother called to tell us that her granddaughter's mother had picked her up and taken her to Michigan. Grandma wanted to know how her granddaughter had gotten out of the school and not been signed out. Good question!

What follows is an unedited letter I received from a concerned parent. The significance of the letter is it gives voice to the suspicion many black parents clearly felt about the school. It also illustrates the gap in education between home and school that some students had to negotiate to be successful in school. There is a significant difference in word acquisition, vocabulary, and language development among low-, middle-, and upper-income groups. For many students from low-income families, it was a steep hill to climb and one of the reasons inner city schools struggle achieving acceptable standardized test scores.

> To Whom It May Concern:
> Since DeMarcus have been in School he never have brought F on his card, but knowing the attitude you white teacher have about the Black children and not only the children but Black, what do you expect. I don't want to have to come up there and take you all to the Board of Education, so I warn you all to stop picking on him.

The principal and I had a meeting with three of our eighth grade teachers to talk about their attitude, general friendliness, cooperation, and team spirit. They saw no problem with their attitude. Since the teachers were more or less arbitrarily assigned to Jefferson, they viewed being at Jefferson as a form of punishment. They all wanted to transfer closer to their homes. Apparently, distance wasn't a factor in the nearby feeder schools. They were not happy campers, and they let everyone know it. Ultimately, they all were transferred to other schools.

The racial issue prevailed. There is a teachers' table in the lunchroom. The white eighth grade teachers would sit together at one end of the teachers' table, and the black eighth grade teachers would sit at the other end. I made it a point to sit with the black teachers in an attempt to loosen up some of the racial barriers. The black teachers solved that problem by not sitting at the table at all. They all sat with their classes. Now, only the white teachers sit at the teachers' table during lunch. At most system-wide meetings, blacks sit on one side of the room and whites on the other. As the years went by, there were many more black principals so that was not noticeable, and I never gave it a thought.

I simply was not prepared for race to have the impact it did, nor the animus I felt from so many black parents, students, and teachers. I had no experience with race when I was growing up. There were some issues in the Marine Corps, but I was a bystander. I tended to think white men exclusively owned racial prejudice. It came as a shock that there was no exclusivity to prejudice. I knew the history and causes of why their feelings existed. I just was not ready for living and working with the reality.

We had a successful open house. The school was packed with parents. One minor incident occurred afterward when three kids, two in high school, raced through the cafeteria kicking over chairs. Jim Griffin and I closed the school and drove over to the Quick Mart where the kids were hanging out. The kids were hostile, particularly one of them. Jim and the very hostile kid stepped behind the store, presumably to talk alone, although the kid was aggressively hostile. The kid came back, chastened, with his jacket dusty and torn. Jim and the kids talked a while longer and then we left. One of their parents showed up the next day to see Jim and left thanking him. Jim had the touch, and after he left education, it turned into the Midas touch.

Dr. Curry in his middle school office

Principal

1983

I think Jim, who I might add was a very good principal, got tired of being a flack catcher as well as dealing with the system's bureaucracy. He resigned, went to work for Valic, and did very, very well. I was appointed principal.

"You had no business talking to my son! It wasn't your business! And I'm getting my lawyer on you!" Saying that, she hung up on me. She was outraged. Her son had come to school badly beaten, and I notified the Department of Human Resources (DHR). They came out and took him into protective custody. I called his mother, who had administered the beating, to inform her of what occurred. That was her response. I thought, *Good luck to you. You'll probably need one.* And as it turned out, she did!

Early in my principalship, I came to work one morning to find a man sitting in my office. He identified himself as a U.S. Marshall who worked in the Witness Protection Program. He was there to enroll the child of someone who was in the Witness Protection Program. It was all very confidential. No one was to know about it other than my secretary and me. We enrolled the child, who attended most of the school year, and never told a soul. Then, one day, they were gone. I think television programs are made out of this stuff.

One of our parents was wheelchair bound. His legs had been amputated. Both of his children constantly got into trouble. His daughter had run away with two other girls after refusing to help her father out of his car. Sadly, his eighth grade daughter had gotten pregnant. She was showing her pregnancy, but her father remained oblivious to it. The school counselor and I went to her house to inform her father of her pregnancy. The dimly lit house had a closed-up dusty feeling. He politely greeted us from his couch. We took a seat in one of the overstuffed chairs. It was an awkward conversation, to say the least. Other than this topic, the father and I had had several contentious conversations about the behavior of his children. At a much later date, the police picked up his seventh grade son for being drunk and for abusing his father. There didn't seem to be a mother around, and I guess the father was doing the best he could with his kids and his handicap. Not a good or healthy situation for anyone involved.

A car hit one of our students on the way to school this morning. The car left the scene of the accident. We called the paramedics and the police. Fortunately, the student was not seriously injured. I don't think the driver was found.

Mr. Jones, a social studies teacher, was a problem. He had been a problem well before I arrived at Jefferson. His personnel file was a good three inches thick. He continually showed up late, seldom turned things in on time, never turned in his plan book with his lessons for the coming week, and rarely did what he was supposed to do. In addition, he let the girls sit on his lap. I wrote a letter notifying him formally not to touch his students. Actually, I wrote several letters. He read the letter to his class. Every time I walked by his classroom, I could hear his students yelling, "Here he comes!"

Eventually, I recommended he be terminated and delivered a copy of the letter to him. He promptly read it to his class. I sent him home. He should have been terminated before I ever got to Jefferson, but other principals simply didn't want to deal with the bureaucracy involved with terminating a teacher. It turned out to be a long and painful school board hearing. It split the faculty, mostly along racial lines. No one doubted that he deserved to be fired, and the board agreed, but that was beside the point when race got involved. As with so much going on in our country, race was the filter through which things tend to be viewed, not right or wrong, good or bad, or fair or unfair.

Jefferson Middle School certainly was not immune to that perception.

Ralph must have been bored, waiting for his mom to pick him up after school. Students were loading the buses when an inspiration struck Ralph. It was his Napoleon Dynamite moment! He turned his back to the buses, dropped his pants, bent over, and mooned the departing buses. It created sensation with the students but didn't go over well with the bus drivers. Ralph's name may have been etched in the annals of school moondom, but it got Ralph into big trouble.

Students continued to call their parents and leave in the middle of our Friday night dance. That was unusual. Normally, the crowd stayed to the bitter end of the dance, and we would wait around while parents slowly straggled in to pick up their children. That wasn't true in this case. Everyone cleared out pretty quickly.

Monday morning, my phone began to ring. "Desmond had a gun at the dance," they said. Desmond was a tall, lanky seventh grader. He should have been in eighth or ninth grade. He was as tall as I was, but he had been held back in elementary school. I started interviewing students, including Desmond, who had been at the dance. They agreed Desmond did bring a gun. They saw the gun. In fact, he had come early to the dance and had popped off a few rounds at the track. Students leaving the dance early were afraid of Desmond. He had a gun, he was bigger and older than they were, and he had a terrible reputation in the community.

After a class III hearing (formal-system-administered hearing), I put Desmond out of school. When time came for Desmond to return to school, I had numerous unhappy parents objecting to his return and threatening to go to Channel 13. Channel 13 had a segment on the news where they investigated various complaints of citizens. It would have been awkward to say the least to have to explain the whole situation to the public.

Our superintendent told us that he wanted to hear of a problem before it hit the news, so I called him. He really gave me an earful when I suggested that Desmond be transferred to another school. Ultimately, Desmond was transferred. I vowed that the next time a problem arose, the superintendent was going to hear it first on the news.

Desmond ended up in juvenile detention, charged with sodomy. His victim, a younger boy, also went to Jefferson. It was another reason for Desmond to be in school elsewhere. I only can imagine how uncomfortable and intimidating it was for Desmond's victim to be in the same school with him. To make it even worse, what Desmond did to this boy was known in the community. Somewhere down the line, Desmond's victim ended up in trouble for a sexual act. My guess is that if you check the statistics, that would fit many victims' profile.

I had another brush with the superintendent. One of my parents acted like a genuine nutcase and, unsurprisingly, had a son constantly in trouble. I had many amicable meetings with this parent about his son's behavior. Predictably, the parent blamed everybody for everything, except his son. Equally predictable, his son's behavior didn't change. Finally, he requested a meeting with the superintendent. My director, the parent, and I all met in the superintendent's office. It turned out to be quite a meeting.

The director and I were sitting near one office wall. Sitting across from the superintendent's desk, the parent began making all kinds of wild accusations. The meeting turned contentious. The superintendent literally could not get in a word.

Finally, the superintendent had enough! Voices were raised and fingers pointed. Tempers were lost. The superintendent leaped up, his chair flying into the wall behind him. The parent picked up his chair and flung it against the opposite wall as they faced off. The tension was palpable. The director and I, astonished at the turn of events, quietly edged our chairs out of the way. The day was saved when security, hearing all the commotion, entered and escorted the parent from the room.

Nonplussed to say the least, the director and I left the building without another word. Sometime later in the day, someone phoned a bomb threat into the board of education. The building had to be evacuated while the police searched for a non-existing bomb. In my mind, it wasn't too hard to figure out who phoned in the bomb threat.

I attended family court today. I met in a room with attorneys, social workers, and police officers. There was a felony indictment against the mother who had severely beaten her child. The mother was a Jehovah's Witness and had literally beaten the devil out of the child. The parent, sticking with her beliefs, showed no remorse, so the prosecution wanted the child out of the house and his mother in jail. The defense opted for a grand jury hearing. Religion aside, many parents had difficulty drawing the line with their children between punishment and abuse. It is an issue that comes up regularly at school.

A student assigned to in-school detention was caught with a beer-rum concoction. He had sneaked into his parents' liquor cabinet and apparently planned to make in-school suspension his happy hour. Rather than getting into the spirits, so to speak, he got an eight-day suspension. And we didn't have to clean up any vomit from overindulgence. Hopefully, his parents will lock their liquor cabinet.

It is spring, and love, or the lack of it, is in the air. One young lady took seven Tylenol because her boyfriend broke up with her. Her mother rushed her to the emergency room. Her former boyfriend, upon hearing about this, ran away from school. He later turned back up. Somehow, the love life of this young lady and her ex-beau became a major concern for a group of eighth grade girls and caused no end of problems. The drama of it all ran rife through the eighth grade halls.

A student had a severe breathing attack. She could not breathe. We called the paramedics. The child was put into Baptist Montclair for one month: the adolescent clinic hysteria unit.

I had a student in my office insisting he had been promoted to eighth grade despite evidence and his former school's principal's statement that he failed three subjects. He made threats to decimate the school if he was retained in seventh grade. We sent him home with his mother for a reality check.

I went out to do an in-house visit this morning. The house was shabby and dirty with The University of Alabama stuff on the walls along with a cheap sword and a club, dirty rug on a dirty floor, and overflowing ashtrays on the table. The beds were unmade, the yard neglected, and the lawn uncut. I talked with the mother about paying for lost books and supervising her son's schoolwork. His mother admitted she wrote excuses to the school when her son played hooky. We had hoped to enlist her help with her son's attendance as well as his schoolwork. The prospects did not look good, nor did her son's future, if he kept playing parent-approved hooky.

An eighth grader hit another eighth grader and was suspended for it. His sister came to pick him up. He lived with his sister because Dad could not control him. He got into a fight with his sister in the office and blows were exchanged. He ran off and then returned. They got into a yelling match in the office, his sister telling him, "Your mother doesn't want you. She doesn't love you." And other things along that line. Sadly, he wasn't the only student living in similar situations.

Camp Cosby

Our National Junior Honor Society (NJHS) was a great success. This mainly was due to the teachers who sponsored it. They did a wonderful job of involving the NJHS in numerous activities. One thing we did was take the NJHS on an overnight trip to Camp Cosby. We started doing this every fall in an effort to provide a little leadership training and to make them feel special for all the hard work it took to make the honor society. On this trip, our bus broke down on the way to Camp Cosby, but we all had a great time. Our NJHS was predominately girls. Good grades were not a badge many boys wanted to wear. Good students who were black males often were called Oreos: white on the inside and black on the outside. It was another example of the influence of peer groups.

Our leadership weekend in the fall with the honor society was built around team building. During the day, we did all kinds of activities requiring teamwork. At night, we slept around an open fire pit. We roasted marshmallows over the fire, told stories, and bedded down for the night. Many of the students had never slept under the stars. One of our girl's father worked in the lunchroom. She was a shy, quiet girl, and he a very protective father extremely reluctant to let his daughter attend. We convinced him to let Ayana come. All the students wore street clothes and brought their bedding to the bonfire prepared for the night. Ayana came in her flannel nightgown, a hair net on her head, wearing fluffy slippers, and carrying her stuffed teddy bear. No one said a word. It was a terrific group.

Our association with Camp Cosby endured over a ten- or twelve-year period. I think we were the first Birmingham City School to start an outdoor education unit. We took our sixth graders to Camp Cosby for a week each spring. Ultimately, we could not get enough chaperones to continue the program. I would end up being the only male. Trying to get a whole bunch of burping, farting, giggling boys to sleep was a real challenge. They had way more energy than I had.

Problems

An eighth grade teacher walked into my office to report that a student, currently absent from school, was pregnant by her father.

"How do you know this?" I asked.

"Well," she said, "The father all but admitted it to Ms. Howard during open house."

"And I am just hearing about this?" I was aghast!

"Ms. Howard was afraid to get involved, but I thought you needed to know," she replied. The student was a pale, quiet, unremarkable girl who blended into the background, avoiding attention.

I contacted the attendance officer, and we drove to the student's house. It was a cinderblock duplex with a small weedy yard on a shaded street. No one was home. We got in touch with the grandmother who told us her grand-daughter was in the hospital.

There were three daughters. One was still in elementary school. I went to see the elementary school principal. She was as appalled as I was about the horrifying turn of events. We talked with the youngest sister who confirmed her sister was pregnant. She had no idea who fathered the baby. She denied her father had done anything inappropriate with her.

We got DHR involved. We also did several drive-bys of the house in an attempt to talk to the father. No one was ever home. I think my student's baby was born with encephalopathy. The older sister also had gotten pregnant and had a baby with a serious medical condition. It was strongly suspected to be the father's baby as well.

As far as I know, a case was never developed against the father. The elementary school principal kept in close contact with her student. At one point, the youngest daughter was going to testify about some inappropriate behavior of her father approaching her for sex. However, she ultimately recanted, so nothing came of it. I never again saw my student. The whole affair left me feeling helpless, outraged, and frustrated. I simply could not imagine a father doing that to his child.

A seventh grader came to school with bruises all over her arms and buttock. Her mother had beaten her over a deficiency note from one of her teachers. We called DHR. The police showed up as well. The DHR worker interviewed her then called her noncustodial father to have her picked up.

One of our girls hit her head on the wall. We called her mother, but the phone was disconnected. We called her mother's work number, but she no longer worked there. We called her emergency number, but her grandmother had nothing to do with her mother. We had to wait until her father came in. This is not an isolated incident. We frequently had a great deal of difficulty reaching a parent. Phone numbers and jobs were often changed with no notification to the school.

We established an intramural sports program. Unfortunately, the boys got too competitive, and fights would break out. For example, one student hit another student during an intramural football game. When coach broke it up, the aggressor gave him the finger and yelled, "Fuck you!" I told the kid to report tomorrow with his mother. He told me to fuck off and then took a swing at me. That landed him in a class III hearing.

He was transferred to another school. The unintended positive consequence resulting from this incident was that he left behind a group of friends who were a negative influence. He fell into a much healthier group in his new school. In middle school, particularly, peer groups play a critical role in what kids choose to do. Sometimes even murder.

13

Teachers

Mr. Miller's class was out of control again. Groan! This was not a new issue! In fact, it was pretty common. Mr. Miller was a last-minute hire from a very diminished pool of applicants. He was a very young fellow, slender, nicely dressed, and just out of college. He came across in our interview as being a little tentative and unsure of himself. In the interview, I asked him how he would handle his discipline. He told me he didn't think he would have a problem because he was bigger than his students. I knew then that trouble was looming, but school had started, and I needed a teacher, so I took a chance.

Kids can sense when blood is in the water. I spent a lot of time in Mr. Miller's classroom. He had zero control of his students. It got to the point on the last day of school before Christmas break that I told him to just keep his students in the room. When next I passed down the hall, Mr. Miller was outside of his room with both hands holding his classroom door closed. If I wasn't so exasperated, I would have felt sorry for him.

In another incident, students were shooting rubber bands in Mr. Miller's class. He bent down to pick one up, and his students took full advantage of the target he presented. It was just too good an opportunity for his students to pass up. He was very upset, but he had no idea who got him in the rear. He certainly wasn't going to get a confession from a class quite pleased with itself.

While we had some excellent teachers, teaching in an inner city school is a very demanding job and not for everyone. Birmingham had a difficult time attracting and keeping talented teachers. Many of our new teachers, right out of college, simply were not prepared to deal with our student population. Others established themselves in the school and, after a year or two, took their experience to more affluent school systems. Over the years, several of my teachers deservedly received recognition by the system and the state for their teaching excellence. Teaching in an inner city school is a really, really tough job. Teachers not only have to make up for the academic deficits of their students but also deal with serious behavioral issues some students bring to school and sometimes what had occurred in a student's community. It truly takes a special person to do it year in and year out. These teachers have, usually unstated, an extremely strong sense of mission. They do not get the recognition or credit they truly deserve.

Frequently, situations did arise that complicated the dynamics of running the school. A teacher gave her two-week notice, leaving everyone in the lurch. Her fiancé had broken off their engagement. So she decided to move to Houston to get away from the situation. As traumatic as the broken engagement was to her, she gave no thought to the thirty students who would have a much less qualified substitute teaching them. The larger mission, the commitment to her students, was forgotten.

I got a call from the wife of one of my teachers to find out if her husband was at work. He wasn't and had no substitute. His wife said he left for work, dropped their daughter at her school, then returned home, and moved out bag and baggage, bed spread included. She later got in touch with me to find out whether he was still working at school. He was. Apparently, he was trying to sell the house without her permission. She said it wasn't the first time he had done this. I have absolutely no idea why she put up with it after the first time.

Another teacher came to my office in tears. She was in the midst of a divorce and having a hard time reigning in her emotions at school. Over the year, she spent a good amount of time in my office, crying over the behavior of her students, her divorce, and friends. Unfortunately, this teacher's emotional issues bled into her classroom and created more problems for everyone involved.

A teacher came to me and said she was thinking of suicide. She had been to the hospital the day before, and they told her to return immediately if those thoughts recurred. She said she was leaving school and going to the hospital. Since any mention of suicide is nothing to take lightly, I strongly endorsed her decision. She was back at work the next day.

A teacher sat in my office one day, telling me of an incident that had occurred several years previously, involving a custodian I had dismissed. The teacher had been working late one afternoon and had gone to the utility closet for a broom. She opened the door, and there was the custodian, pants around his ankles, standing in front of a seated female assistant custodian. "Oh!" she said. "Excuse me." Quickly shutting the door, she fled back to her room. She never reported it. I can only surmise that in her mind it was, after all, a utility closet. No teacher wants to upset a custodial worker. They are far too helpful to teachers in a myriad of ways.

The only son of this female assistant custodian was killed in a neighborhood shooting. I attended numerous viewings/funerals involving staff, or students, throughout the years. Tragedy seemed to stalk so many of them.

Issues with teachers were as various and compelling as were those of students. All of it came through the principal's desk, often presenting a challenge. At times, they confided to me about different things in their lives. That they were comfortable to do so, I took as a compliment. One teacher, though, certainly changed my life.

Freda

It was another hot, muggy summer day. I was toiling in my office. A knock at the door and in walks this really attractive, shapely young lady in short white shorts that set off her tan legs. She immediately got my attention.

"Hi, Dr. Curry. I am Freda Fox, your new special education teacher."

Whoa, I thought. *All right! The summer is looking up!*

What I said was "Let me show you your classroom." Her classroom actually was a trailer.

I spent a lot of time that summer helping her in her classroom. Well, she worked, I observed, providing a running commentary in my most sagacious manner. She had a great personality and a wonderful sense of humor. She laughed a lot, and it was contagious. I was smitten.

Ah, alas. I pontificate while she works is another quality she claims has remained over the years. In my opinion, there is something to be said for consistency.

Freda was raised on a small farm in Hanceville, Alabama. Her high school was the first integrated school in Cullman County. The Ku Klux Klan was still active in Cullman County. Freda had several black friends. One night, she got a call from the KKK, telling her to stay away from the black students, or they would burn a cross on her lawn. The KKK also showed up at her senior bonfire in full regalia, robes, hoods, and all, and told all the black students to leave.

In many respects, Freda's parents represented those early farmers who were the backbone of America. They were, in essence, subsistence farmers who worked from dawn to dusk, clearing land and growing a variety of crops. They were fundamentalists, believing the word of the Bible as written: good or bad, no gray area, no interpretation. Freda got their work ethic and her mother's Biblical absoluteness. God knows, figuratively and literally, how she ended up with me, by all measures a heathen. She remains convinced that when the rapture comes, I will be left behind. And she told me she was taking our dog! That was a blow! I, at least, was hoping for our dog!

Freda had taught disadvantaged children in a tough part of New Orleans. She really had the knack for creating a rapport with her students. She always seemed to be able to get the best from them. She demanded their best and would accept nothing less. If a student fell down on the job, she and the student stayed late until the job was done. It was not unusual to find her working with a recalcitrant student well after 6 p.m. Their parents became her staunchest supporters. They knew she cared about their child and that was what every parent wanted most for their child. This was particularly true of special education children who sometimes got shunted aside.

She did well with difficult students. She delighted in telling stories on herself. In another school, she was dealing with a very hyperactive student. Finally, she had enough. She turned from what she was doing on blackboard and, in her sternest voice, thoroughly dressed the boy down for his behavior.

When she turned again from the blackboard, he was on the floor on his hands and knees under a table. Looking fierce, hands on her hips, she demanded, "What are you doing, crawling around down there!"

Innocently, he looked up at her, "I'm looking for my self-esteem."

That was too funny. It cracked her up. She simply couldn't keep a straight face. Her kids loved her.

Another time, she had to go into the hall as one of her students was rolling around on the floor, yelling and flailing his arms. He had gotten into an argument that turned into a fight with his imaginary friend. Freda had to break it up. His imaginary friend was named Sid, and this wasn't the first time Freda had to break up a fight between her student and Sid. Apparently, the student and Sid had a complicated relationship.

As it turned out, in addition to being a terrific teacher and after a five-year courtship as well as her moving to a school outside our system, she became my wife. I guess being a special education teacher, she felt she was well suited for that job.

Originally, we planned to get married in a picturesque wedding chapel in Gatlinburg, but I chickened out. We ended up getting married at the Jefferson County Courthouse by an old, disheveled minister with food on his tie. Not very romantic but mission accomplished. Afterward, we drove to the Fort McClellan's Post Exchange. Freda continues to claim that was our honeymoon. I categorically deny it!

Confrontation

My secretary, standing in the parking lot, was frantically waving at me as I arrived back to school after taking lunchroom money to the bank. She said that the assistant principal needed my help with an angry parent. She didn't mention that the parent was angry with me. I walked into a hornet's nest. The parent had a violent temper and was yelling and screaming at us. Well, really at me. His brother was there with him. They both were way bigger than I was and, for a while, I thought I might be going out the window. The father was angry because I had paddled his son for spitting in a girl's food. What really upset him was that on a previous incident, he had shown up at school, intending to paddle his son in front of the class. I wouldn't let him. I told him he had to paddle his son at home, not in front of the class. I asked them to leave. They wouldn't. Normally, if a parent refused to leave my office, I would leave. With no one to talk at, the parent would walk out. These men were standing in front of the door, venting their anger. Leaving was not an option. Ultimately, we had to call the police and have the parent and his brother escorted out of the building.

There was a sigh of relief as they exited. The tension that filled the room abated. I'm thinking, *Maybe I ought to take karate.*

The school was broken into over the weekend. They got into the office and took about $10 from the petty cash box. Unfortunately, this was not an isolated incident. Usually, computers, televisions, and video recorders were taken. This also happened at Franklin Elementary School when I was principal there. We would get a new riding lawnmower, secure it in a locked shed, and it would be stolen within a month or so. We also continually had our copper wire taken. The thieves seldom seemed to get caught.

One morning, I came to work to find my bottom desk drawer missing. The outer office had not been touched, just my desk drawer. I couldn't figure out how the intruders got into my office. I looked everywhere. No sign of the break in, only my missing drawer. Some days later, the windowpane in my office fell in. It turned out they removed a windowpane and crawled through the opening. When they left, they replaced the pane. They were smooth. Maybe not their first break in. I am pretty sure who did it, but I have no evidence. I took a knife away from a student. He wanted it back. Apparently, that was his special knife. I wouldn't give it to him. He not only took the knife, he took the whole drawer. It contained numerous confiscated items, including a magnificently contoured black rubber phallus of significant proportions. The bus driver who turned it in to me said the kids were having a great time waving it around in the back of the bus. No doubt.

The counselor came in to talk about a student who confided that after school she kept her two-year old brother until 9 p.m. every weekday and on weekends. Sometimes her mother did not come home at all. She also had caught her mother having sex in the living room with her boyfriend. Like many students, this child assumed adult responsibilities for a negligent parent.

We called DHR several times the last few days. Mostly it was because a student would come to school with marks, welts, and bruises on them from their mother or, frequently, her boyfriend. Invariably, someone in the household would lose his or her temper and hit the kid with a fist or beat them with an extension cord, belt, or something else that would leave a mark. Some of our kids were beaten pretty badly.

One of our students came to school with a fat lip and bite marks on her hand. She had gotten into a fight with her mother. Her mother held her down, slapped her in the face, and bit her finger. Her mother had a history of drugs. No father in evidence.

A couple of boys came to school drunk. They threw up all over the place. I doubt the suspension was nearly as painful as their hangover.

Four eighth grade boys jumped another boy. They got him down and kicked him, bruising, and scraping his ribs. I suspended the four boys. One of their parents complained that I suspended four black boys and no white boys. Well, that was because it was four black boys who did it. I have noticed that any fight attracts a crowd, and whenever one of the participants goes down, everyone else jumps in and starts kicking him. No chivalry in this crowd. The days of one on one, taking it to the parking lot are long gone.

I got word that two of our boys were arrested. They were riding on a stolen motorbike, breaking into houses.

We have six substitute teachers in the building today. I expect it to be a very busy day for the assistant principal and me.

I had a talk with Demarco about driving his truck to school. He had an old rattletrap pickup and would arrive at school each morning with a truck full of kids. Demarco was about five feet tall and around 300 lbs., a great middle guard with some unexplored questions regarding his eligibility. He was one of the several sixteen- or seventeen-year-old eighth graders. They were too old in my opinion to be in middle school. Jefferson Middle School had ten- or eleven-year-old sixth graders. This happenstance resulted from their inability in elementary school to pass the Birmingham

Essential Skills Test. Most of these students were special ed students who had not been identified in elementary school.

Demarco solved the transportation problem by parking across the street from the school. He still brought a load of kids to school from his neighborhood. Demarco was well thought of by his teachers. They thought him a big affectionate teddy bear. The football coach loved him. He was stout on the defensive line. Sadly, as an adult, he got involved in a weird love triangle and ended up in prison for murder.

Spring holidays are about to begin. We called police to be on hand the last day. There were persistent rumors that the Disciples, a west end gang, were going to show up. Also, on the last day, cars tend to get vandalized, so it never hurt to have the police around.

A parent came in to tell me she was getting a divorce. She was afraid her child's father would take her child from school. That got complicated if both parents were on record as being able to check the child out of school. It took a court order or divorce decree to restrict a parent from a child. The school, at times, got caught in the middle of a parental dispute.

We had two sisters who said they were afraid to go home to their aunt with whom they lived. We notified DHR. They went home with their grandfather.

We found a knife on a student that had been taken in a burglary. A gun had also been taken, but we did not find it. The student's father was in prison for drugs.

A seventh grader was threatening suicide because other kids were making fun of her and asking if she was a virgin.

Her mother had beaten her, and her uncle had raped her when she was five years old. We met with her father to discuss the issues and encourage him to seek help for her. It was another sad story in a whole list of sad stories we dealt with.

Substitutes

A student came running into my office. "Dr. Curry, they need you on the sixth grade hall! Hurry!"

I could hear the commotion before I ever arrived. One of the classroom doors was open. I could see desks overturned and pencils and scissors thrown around on the floor. Standing in front of the class, finger pointing wildly about, the substitute was ranting at the class about their behavior. Before he could throw anything else or do any more damage, I got into the room and calmed him down. Apparently, he had fortified himself with alcohol before arriving to substitute. He reeked of it. I escorted him out the door and sent him home. He needed to sleep it off. I called personnel and had them remove him from the substitute list.

Being a substitute teacher is a hard job. Certainly not a job suited for everyone. Even normally well-behaved students tend to view a substitute teacher as an opportunity to misbehave. In another incident, I got called to a class to find our science teacher holding back a very angry substitute teacher who was trying to get after a student. In an effort to control his class, he told them he was a Vietnam veteran and held a fifth-degree black belt so they had better not mess with him. Of course, that merely presented a challenge to the more precocious students. I sent him home too.

One of our substitutes was having no problem with student discipline. She was in a trailer, showing a video on a television set up in front of her desk. She couldn't see the screen. The kids kept giggling and snickering. Every time the substitute got up and looked at the television, the students changed the channel. The substitute got suspicious and called for a regular teacher. When the students saw the teacher coming, they slipped the tape out of the machine and started passing it back as the teacher went down the row. The last guy had no one to pass it to. It turned out they were watching a XXX-rated movie someone had brought to school. Amazingly, I received no calls from parents regarding the movie. Apparently, the students were staying mum. The movie probably belonged to one of the parents, and they certainly were staying mum!

We had a substitute show up in full drag. I had never in my life seen a man in full drag: hair, skirt, stockings, blouse, shoes, earrings, jewelry, the works. I was flabbergasted! Keeping a straight face was nearly impossible. The secretary and I had to step out into the hall until we could regain our composure. None of us were quite prepared for the outfit. He was assigned to an emotionally conflicted class of about eight to ten students. We never heard a peep from those students who could at times be very difficult. They worked diligently throughout the day. When he came into the lunchroom with the class, the lunchroom fell dead quiet. I guess he inspired awe. Much later, he showed up as a substitute in my next school, only this time dressed as a man. He was quite a nice person. We simply had never been exposed to someone who was so different, at least in this manner. Sadly, he was murdered, and the perpetrator was never found.

One of my most bizarre incidents involved a substitute physical education teacher hired for the year. One day, she didn't show up for work. No message. Nothing. We tried but failed to contact her. Weeks went by. Then one day, she showed back up and resumed work as if she hadn't missed a day.

"What happened?" I asked. "Where were you?"

Unperturbed, she said, "I was kidnapped."

"Kidnapped!" I exclaimed. I'd never met anyone who had been kidnapped. The whole thing sounded odd. Particularly since she didn't seem in the least upset. No police came around to investigate it either.

A few months later, she disappeared again! When she reappeared, I asked, "Where have you been?"

Without turning a hair, she said, "I was kidnapped again."

Again! That tore the fabric of any credibility. Who gets kidnapped twice? We got another physical education teacher. Her next kidnapping was going to be on her own time!

Murder

I called a parent for a conference concerning her son. She refused to come to school. Following this student's matriculation to high school, he got involved with a bad group. They kidnapped a woman, stripped her, murdered her, and cut her up. They were caught because this student brought one of her fingers to school to show around. He kept it as a souvenir in a little tin box. All the boys involved are serving life sentences in prison.

A student came to school, acting very lethargic with bloodshot eyes. He said he had a hangover. I called to inform his mother. She said she sent him to school with a hangover to teach him a lesson. Fortunately, he didn't get sick in class, or at least sick enough to throw up.

One of our students who had been missing showed up at school. His mother had no idea of where he had gone and had notified Youth Aide Missing Person. He ran off again as soon as his mother came to school. Eventually, his mother sent him to Detroit to get away from the gangs he was running with. He was murdered in Detroit. His younger brother, whom one of our teachers had taken under her wing, also was murdered here in Birmingham. They were gang-related murders. The teacher was greatly affected by the younger brother's death. She had worked hard to gain his trust and try to help him have a better life. His murder came as an absolute shock to her. I think she thought she had helped him get away from that influence. She was a terrific teacher, the kind we so desperately needed. She subsequently chose to work in a more affluent school system. She had spent a great deal of her emotional capital with this child.

Another student we caught coming to school with an iron bar. I am not sure what he was planning, but it wasn't good. After finishing middle school, this student ended up in jail for murder. His older brother was already in jail for murdering someone, and I think his younger brother was murdered, or involved in murder too. Sadly, after leaving middle school, a number of our students were murdered, or ended up in jail for murder.

Two former Jefferson students in high school murdered another of our former students. I have no idea why. He was a sweet, inoffensive kid. It is hard to understand how these kids get themselves in situations where they are murdered, or they commit murder. Any time would be bad, but it seemed to happen way too often with our former students. In a very large number of cases, the boys had no father in the home to provide a role model of healthy behavior, and mother couldn't always cope with their son's behavior.

A very upset parent called because she said one of the seventh grade teachers got in her son's face, pointed her finger, and asked if he wanted to fight. The parent insisted she was coming to school tonight to confront the teacher. I told her that tonight would not be a good time for a conference because we had open house. There was limited time to talk with teachers. I suggested she, the teacher, and I have a conference at any other time. I told her the assistant principal and I had trouble with her son's insolence. The parent persisted in saying she would get this taken care of tonight. I again explained that it would not be an appropriate time and again, suggested a conference at another time. The parent heatedly insisted she would deal with the teacher tonight. Finally, I told her that if there were a problem tonight, I would ask her to leave and call the police. After more heated words from her and with me trying to invite her to a conference at another time, she hung up on me. As an adult, her son was murdered in a drug deal. He was shot through the door of his apartment. His mother became an elementary school teacher.

Special Education

Well, this is a new one. One of our special ed teachers brought one of her students to the office. She said he kept repeatedly running around her classroom without his pants and attempting to mount the leg of the special ed aide. I can't say I had any good suggestions. I did tell him to keep his pants on and zipped up.

The truth is that I had some really good special ed teachers who capably handled a variety of issues. We also had some excellent special education students, some of whom were regularly on the honor roll and in the honor society. Special education encompasses a wide range of disabilities.

Some of the things the special education teachers handled you couldn't make up. This is a conversation between the same special ed teacher and one of her students as he pulled up his shirt and down his pants, "Look, Ms. Paul, I've got diabetes."

Unfazed, Ms. Paul to the student, "No, Charlie, you are sweating." Charlie wasn't sweating. He had, had an ejaculation. Well, I guess you could call it sweating.

The next day, he came with some tablets. He told Ms. Paul his mother gave them to him to take when his puberty started acting up. Thirty minutes into the period, Charlie's puberty started acting up, and he asked to take a pill. Ms. Paul took a look at the situation, observed that, in fact, his puberty was acting up, and told Charlie to go take his pill.

I got a message from the assistant principal to come to the lunchroom. Outside the lunchroom, one of our special education students was pacing up and down. He was agitated and out of control. He was angry because his "evil ancestors were talking to me." I told him I had the same problem. That got him even angrier. "You just think I'm crazy. Don't touch me!" Okay, I shouldn't have said I had the same problem, but if this kept up, I might.

We called his mother but got no answer. We called his emergency number and got no answer there either but left a message. We called the special ed coordinator. She told us he was big, violent, angry, and crazy, and he hears voices. Well, we had worked that out ourselves. She also said he had molested a girl and still slept with his mother. His father was dead. Eventually, we defused the situation and calmed him down.

Our male special ed teacher, a big, burly, and very proper guy who played football in college, came to the office a little shaken. Two of his rather large girls got into a fight. One of them ripped the blouse and bra off of the other girl. When the teacher charged into the middle of the fray to break it up, he got hit smack in the face with a naked boob. Surprised, shocked, he jumped back, saying, "Back, girl. Back!" He was out of his depth there.

One of our special education students was sent to the office for mooning the class. He gave the assistant principal a false name and phone number. The assistant principal called the wrong parents and told them to come to school and pick up their child. In the meantime, he asked to go to class to get his books. When the assistant principal sent him, he ran off. He reappeared later, and there was a rumor that he had a gun and was going to kill the assistant principal.

We checked him and found no gun. However, the next day, a neighbor reported that the student had been in his car and had stolen his pistol. We got statements from other students testifying that he had stolen the pistol. I called the principal at Adam's Elementary School, who obtained a statement from his younger brother. A class III hearing was held. He admitted mooning the class but denied having the gun. His parents sided with him despite five witnesses testifying that he did have the gun. I told him it was a federal crime to have a gun at school, and I would pursue it with the police if he didn't turn up that gun by the next day. That really upset his parents, and they stormed out of the meeting. I didn't get the gun. I doubt his parents would have turned it in even had they found it. He was placed in the alternative school with the appropriate individual education plan.

One of our female emotionally conflicted students met two of her classmates in the bushes. One of the students was her brother. She pulled down her pants and squatted so that one of the boys could insert his finger into her vagina. The other boy, her brother, was an interested observer. The girl had a history of sexual abuse or acts. She did the same thing in elementary school. Sexual abuse seemed to be another common thread among the issues I encountered over the years.

14

Desert Storm

January 1991

I was freezing my ass off. I arrived at Fort Bragg, North Carolina, on a dark December evening, mobilized with my unit for Desert Storm. Having just joined the unit, I hadn't been issued a warm jacket. I was the COMSEC (communication security) custodian in-charge of all the secret and top-secret codes the 20th Special Forces Group used to communicate. New at the job, I took the codes from the vault in the Birmingham armory and dumped them all into boxes for transportation to Fort Bragg. No inventory, nothing. I hadn't a clue.

I had been feeling restless. I loved the military and took great pride in my time in the Marine Corps. Freda encouraged me to look into the National Guard as a way to keep my job while having a part-time military affiliation. First, I checked in the Marine Corps reserves. I had been out of the military for twenty years. The Marine Corps said that was too long for me to get back my commission.

I ended up joining the Alabama National Guard where I was appointed a chief warrant officer. Ironically enough, my appointment was based on my disastrous training as telecommunication crewman. No telephone pole climbing required.

I went to warrant officer school at Fort Gordon, Georgia, to learn to be a communication specialist. I was totally out of touch with the Army jargon and equipment. They had acronyms for everything, and I didn't know any of them. I struggled. I was the most educated and least prepared member of my class. Fortunately, I was better prepared when I went back as a member of the 20th Group for the senior warrant officers school, finishing at the top of my class. Serendipity, I made friends with another COMSEC custodian who really knew his business. He took the time to help me set up my codes so everything was organized and accounted for. That was no small matter when dealing with top-secret material. It kept me out of what could have been a lot of hot water.

I first was assigned to a computer unit in Montgomery but that really wasn't my cup of tea. I interviewed with, and was accepted in, the 20th Special Forces Group. *That was my cup of tea.* I would have preferred to be an operator, but the days of that level of physical fitness were long gone. I became their COMSEC custodian: the keeper of the codes. My place of business was a large walk-in vault. I had a top-secret / sensitive compartmented information security clearance. It was a highly information sensitive job.

I no sooner had gotten into the 20th Group, then Desert Storm broke out. We were mobilized and sent to

Fort Bragg for further training. Before we were deployed to Iraq, the war ended. While most of the group was sent home, I went to jump school at Fort Benning.

Now that was an experience! I was forty-nine years old and referred to by the instructors as Geritol (a dietary supplement frequently used by seniors). It wasn't a nickname I would have preferred. We ran everywhere all day and practiced jumping off a variety of objects, learning how to do a parachute landing fall (PLF), hitting the ground without breaking any bones. Everyone was much younger than I, and every evening, I would get into the hot tub at the officers' club. Everything ached. There was a big run at the end of each week. If you fell out of the run, you were dropped from the school. You weren't just dropped, you were made to stand by the side of the road as everyone ran by, waving at you and chanting, "Bye. Bye. Bye. Bye." That certainly provided some incentive to stick with it.

The most exciting time at the school was jump week. In that week, trainees made five jumps in order to receive their parachute wings. I was a little nervous, which is something of an understatement. We went to a big shed where we all were issued parachutes. These parachutes were used over and over with each succeeding class. The parachute I was issued had a yellow tag attached. I thought for sure the yellow tag indicated a damaged parachute they had mistakenly given to me. I went back to the issue point and tried to return it as defective, but they were having none of it and, no doubt, thoroughly enjoying my obvious discomfort. Well, I wasn't seeing the humor. I didn't like high places to begin with, and the possibility of an inoperable parachute really gave me the willies.

Sitting on the web benches of a crowded aircraft with my yellow-tagged parachute, I definitely was feeling anxious. The jumpmaster was up near the aircraft door.

He started his ritual, yelling, "Outboard personnel, stand up!" We all stood up as we echoed each of his commands.

"Hook up!" He mimed each command as we hooked our static line to the cable running the length of the aircraft.

"Check equipment!" Everyone checked his own equipment and that of the person in front of him.

"Sound off equipment check!" The person in the rear taps the person in front of him, yelling, "Okay!" It goes down the line until it reached the jumpmaster. Another jumpmaster walked down the line, checking each jumper.

An aircraft crewman opened the aircraft door and kicked out the step for the jumpers. Wind from the opened door roared in our ears. He and the jumpmaster checked around the door for obstacles.

"Three minutes!" The jumpmaster sang out, holding up three fingers.

"Stand in the door!" The lead jumper moved in front of the door as the line of jumpers closed up behind him.

The light next to the door changes from red to green.

"Go! Go! Go! Go!" The jumpmaster yelled.

Jumpers handed their static line to the jumpmaster and disappeared out the aircraft door. Once the line of jumpers began to move, everyone was swept along with it. There was no opportunity for second thoughts.

Fortunately for me, when I stepped out the door of the aircraft at 1,250 feet, everything worked perfectly. I actually got to the point that I liked jumping, especially with my unit. Exiting a fixed wing C130 or a C141 is entirely different from exiting a helicopter. On a C130, the airman opens the door and kicks out a step. The wind created by the slip stream blasts by the door as jumpers file rapidly down the fuselage, hand their static line to the jumpmaster, step out the door, and are literally blown away. It is a violent exit.

On a CH47 or CH53 helicopter, the jumper stands at the end of the ramp with a view of the countryside and the tiny images below. He literally steps out into space, plunging down in silence, counting, "One thousand one. One thousand two," then the opening shock as the parachute catches air and brings the plunge to an abrupt halt. That first step into space high above the ground is what stays with me. It is a leap of faith that my parachute will work properly, and perhaps, a test of courage. Adrenalin is surging.

In either case, after checking to make sure no other jumper is so near he could collapse my chute, I would get a few minutes to enjoy the view and the stillness before trying to guide the parachute to a suitable landing spot and prepare for the inevitable thump upon landing. For a few years, I would take a group of students from the middle school on a field trip to Fort Benning. We would eat in the mess hall and tour the National Infantry Museum. I would take the opportunity to jump with one of the airborne classes while our students would sit in the stands and watch the whole operation. I think the field trip was a good experience for our students. When I was able to get a jump worked in for me, it helped offset some of my more frustrating days at school.

One of my more memorable jumps happened at Fort Bragg. A former student was a member of the 82nd Airborne Division. We arranged to do a night jump together. We met at the green ramp where all the airborne operations at Fort Bragg initiate and boarded an Air Force plane, practicing a nap-of-the-earth airdrop. Nap-of-the-earth is a low altitude flight course using geographical contours to avoid enemy radar. And, for the uninitiated, a great way to get airsick!

The plane was packed with a Humvee and several large crates. No room for seats. We were strapped in on the floor of the fuselage near the front of the aircraft. The ramp in the back of the aircraft was closed. Absolute darkness descended. The aircraft crew had night-vision goggles. Everything was green to them. We had nothing. Everything was pitch black to us. The plane sped along, skimming up and down terrain features. It was a very bumpy ride. My stomach was doing flip-flops. The plane popped up in altitude, the ramp came down, and out went some of the equipment. The ramp closed, and down we went for more nap-of-the-earth. Up again to jump altitude, and down came the ramp. The crewman, wearing his night-vision goggles, guided us like blind men around equipment and to the end of the ramp. As far as I was concerned, our parachute equipment check was way too cursory, but there we were, looking out at a black void. In the distance, I could see lights from the town. Looking down, I could see nothing. One step, and we were falling through space, wrapped in a cocoon of ink, surrounded by stillness. I couldn't see the ground, so my main concern became being prepared when I hit dirt.

We landed none the worse for wear. Our adrenaline was surging. The young man I jumped with, normally a quiet fellow, couldn't stop talking. I don't know if he had ever stepped off the ramp of a C130. Normally, the 82nd goes out the door of an aircraft. Going out the door, you are out before you know it. Stepping off the ramp in daylight highlights the panorama and your height.

When the military released me from active duty, I returned to my day job at school. I was greeted with much enthusiasm even by some teachers who may not have been in my fan club. The lady who had taken my place during the months I was on active duty had managed to alienate virtually everyone with whom she had come into contact. The first thing that she had done was clean out my office, and in the process, she had gotten rid of two valued paintings: one that I brought from Vietnam, and one a grateful grandmother had painted and given to me. I found that inexcusable. I was angry, to say the least. The upside was that I had some very cooperative, even eager, teachers for a while.

CW3 Curry preparing for an equipment jump as
a member of the 20th Special Forces.

Shaniqua

Virtually the first thing I saw when I walked out of my office was Shaniqua haul off and slap a spindly little sixth grader. Shaniqua, a solidly built seventh grader, had a mean streak that already had landed her in three separate detention facilities. She was a force to be reckoned with. We were working with her, but it was an uphill battle. She was very noncompliant. An understatement at the very least!

I ordered her to go to the office. She was having none of it. Reeking attitude, she tossed her head, informed me that I could "kiss her muthafuckin' ass," turned on her heels, and stomped off. *Ah.* I was beyond angry. I trailed her down the hall until I finally I got her into the office where she proceeded to do nothing I told her to do except reinforce her directive to "Kiss her muthafuckin' ass!" We had her mother come and pick her up.

My wife never tires of hearing about this incident. Especially the part where Shaniqua tells me to "Kiss her muthafuckin' ass." It always elicits a chuckle. I suspect there is an ulterior motive in play.

Some days later, the assistant principal and I were chatting as we watched students board the busses to go home. Shaniqua appeared, got in line, and entered one of the busses. She was suspended. She shouldn't have been there, much less riding a bus home. We looked at each other.

"Well," I said, "we could go over and throw her off the bus. It would create a big scene. She, no doubt, would tell us to 'kiss her muthafuckin' ass,' or we could let her get home and call her mother to make sure she doesn't come back." Not much of a decision there. We agreed that discretion was the better part of valor.

Shaniqua was an entrepreneur. Apparently, in the mornings before school, she would wait at the store across the street. The boys would pool their money. Shaniqua would go behind the store and service the boy with the most money.

I got a call from Shaniqua's mother saying the police had picked up Shaniqua. The mother had come home to find Shaniqua's five-year-old brother performing oral sex on her. That was the last straw for the mother! She called the police. We have heard nothing of Shaniqua since. I suspect she is making life interesting in another detention facility.

Potpourri

His behavior was awful. A reedy washed-out-looking kid with a crowded mouth full of misshapen yellow teeth. In all likelihood, his teeth had never been brushed. His breath reeked of decay. He was an angry kid, constantly railing against authority. His eighth grade English teacher and her church group agreed to sponsor his much-needed dental work. After school, I would take him to the UAB dental school, and his English teacher would see that he got home. At times, I took him home. In the unkempt backyard of a house badly in need of a paint job lurked three or four sleek, obviously well-cared-for thoroughbred Doberman Pinschers. The parent's priorities seemed obvious, and it didn't take a degree in psychology to work out the root of some of his anger. After his dental work, his English teacher's church group wanted to sponsor braces, but he would have none of it. His anger continued to manifest itself in his misconduct and focus on his teachers and me.

Each day had a rhythm to it, beginning with early morning bus duty and culminating as the last student left school at the end of the school day. But the unexpected always lurked just around the corner, ready to disrupt the tempo of the day. That unpredictability contributed to the appeal for working in a middle school. Complacency was not an option.

A student put his arm through a classroom window. I have no idea how he did it or why, but there was blood everywhere! I couldn't get in touch with his parents. I didn't want him to bleed to death, so I put him in my car and rushed him to Children's Hospital. He got seventeen stitches.

A student was caught stealing ice cream in the lunchroom. The mother remained hostile until the kid confessed.

A parent wants an appointment with my director and me. Their son was suspended because of numerous discipline referrals.

A father came in upset because a sixth grade teacher sent home a message for another child via his daughter. It included a threat if the message was not delivered. I talked to the teacher about the appropriateness on using a student to deliver her message.

A mother came to school at 4 p.m. upset because her son was suspended for misbehaving in in-school suspension. The mother was very emotional and in tears. She was at her wits end on how to deal with her son. There was no father in the home.

A father was distraught, in tears. He said he could not control his daughter. He said she was having sex with older boys and that she likes gang bangs. I didn't have much advice to offer. He should be talking to a licensed counselor. I simply couldn't fathom how things could get to this point in a family. What kind of family dynamics were involved? Was there a mother in the house?

A parent came by to report that one of our students had threatened his son with a knife. We got the other boy in the office and found two knives on him.

A parent reported their son was taken to the UAB adolescent center. He had a bad weekend. He was caught in a girl's apartment and shot in the head with a BB gun by the girl's father. It could have been worse. It might not have been a BB gun.

The police came to school to pick up a student for sodomy, "deviant sexual intercourse by forcible compulsion." That was how the pick-up order read. It is hard for me to understand how kids get in these situations. In some cases, these kids come from healthy homes, but for the most part, their home is dysfunctional.

Brian is in my office again. This is the third time this week his teacher has sent him. Brian really is more annoying than a discipline problem. I think his teacher's patience is at an end. She isn't the only one. I am seeing the same kids sent to my office for fairly minor disciplinary reasons more often. Problems teachers would have handled themselves earlier in the year. Summer is just around the corner. Teachers are tired. I am tired. The unrelenting drumbeat of situations large and small is wearing. Students are ready for the school year to be over.

Everyone looks forward to summer. It is a time to regenerate. I view the school year in terms of a reservoir. Every fall, we would begin school with our reservoir brimming with hope, energy, and enthusiasm. The arrival of the Christmas break would find our reservoir nearing half full. Issues developing as the school year progresses temper some of our hope, enthusiasm, and energy. By May, our reservoir is low. The continuing issues and constant need to maintain a positive approach to the multitude of problems presented throughout the year is wearing. A summer of workshops and some leisure time refill our reservoir with hope, energy, and enthusiasm, allowing us to greet each new school year brimming with excitement.

I always loved the fall and the beginning of the new school year. Fall came with cooler weather, football season, Thanksgiving, and Christmas holidays. There were a whole series of events for teachers to build lessons around and for students to get excited about. It also was an opportunity for students to renew friendships and make new ones after a long hot summer at home. Each new school year, I got to implement the plans I so conscientiously made during the summer. I was organized. I always had great plans. Of course, they went south in short order once the school year began, but we always started out well organized and comprehensive. After that, it frequently turned into quick improvisation based on our original plans.

I organized the school into houses with portions of each grade level in different houses. I picked up the idea from some of my British friends with whom I played rugby. Many of their schools used a house system as a method of organizing the school. It lent itself to school competitions and creating esprit de corps within each house. Unfortunately, these were the days before Harry Potter, and no one, teachers and students included, had a clue of how a house system worked. It never really evolved into what I had in mind. I had conceived of each house composed of sixth through eighth graders, competing in spelling bees, academic bowls, athletic competitions, etc. The only activity that got off the ground was the athletic competitions. All too frequently, that competition became too intense, and we would have to step in to avoid a fight. Brawling definitely was not one of our chosen sports.

I also designed a rotating schedule so students wouldn't have the same class at the same time each day. A class like math would be taught in the morning some days and later in the day on other days. This optimized teaching and learning times. I had charts in the hallway detailing which day and time each subject was taught. Teachers worked to keep it straight. Students picked it up right away.

We were sitting in a courtyard at Julia Tutwiler Prison for Women, listening to a young lady tell us her story. It was pretty riveting. As she told it, "I was just out for a ride with my boyfriend. He said he needed cigarettes, so we stopped at a convenience store. I didn't know he was going to rob the store!"

He robbed the store and, in the process, murdered the clerk. The police arrested both of them for murder. She was tried and sentenced to a long prison term. Hers was not an isolated story. We heard similar stories from other inmates.

I took several groups to tour the prison and to hear from some of the inmates. I wanted to graphically emphasize the importance of making good decisions, choosing friends wisely, and possible consequences for not doing so.

It was an eye opener for students and teachers alike. The women slept on closely spaced steel framed cots in a large open room. Male and female guards supervised all areas of the prison, including bathroom and shower facilities. No privacy anywhere. Women walked from their sleeping area to their various daytime activities.

We got a peek at death row. A guard sat at a desk in front of several cells. One of the cells was occupied, but we could not see the occupant. A death row inmate got one hour of exercise, by herself, out of her cell a day.

Prison: the lack of privacy, the confinement for years at a time, the regimentation in Spartan living conditions all had an impact. It provided a load of classroom teaching moments about the law, value systems, choosing good friends, and making good choices. They were topics sorely in need of exploring.

Anger

"Ms. Pickens, can I talk to you?" That was how it started, like many similar instances involving our school counselor. Then hesitantly, amid tears, the story poured out. After listening to her story, Ms. Pickens talked with me and notified DHR and the police.

The police report read as follows:

> Officer responded to call to Jefferson Middle School. R.P. (Reporting Person) school counselor expressed concern about a student, victim who states that she is being both verbally and physically abused. Victim stated her mother has abused her constantly. Victim stated that over the past 3 or 4 yrs., since her grandfather's death, her mother shoves her into objects, slaps her about the face & body, punches her and kicks her in the stomach.
>
> Victim also states that her mother constantly calls her a fuck-up and curses her out. According to victim, both her parents have drug problems and they, along with their friends, smoke marijuana about nine times per week. Victim also stated that her mother was abused as a child and has seen a therapist in the past.
>
> Victim also says her step brother has attempted running away several times

before finally leaving upon turning 18 because of sexual, verbal & physical abuse. The brother is now living in Gainesville, FL with victim's aunt where he is now seeking therapy.

Victim stated that her father is an alcoholic and does nothing to stop the abuse. Victim lives with both parents and a three-year-old adopted sister. Victim also showed officer a mark on top of her left hand caused by her mother pushing her into a kitchen counter. Victim also had two scars on her left wrist which victim stated she caused herself during two separate suicide attempts. R.P. has notified DHR and has also been in touch with victim's aunt and brother Christopher in Gainesville.

A common theme throughout seems to be parents' inability to handle their anger. That trait is passed right down to their children. Corporal punishment appears to be the only kind of punishment they use on their children. Anger and corporal punishment are not a good combination. The failure of parents to check their anger serves as a poor model for their children.

An eighth grade boy was upset with a girl who, he said, put her finger in his cake. He did not tell his teacher or me. He got the girl in the hall, hit her, and knocked her into the glass trophy case, breaking the glass. His mother said the girl had provoked the incident and deserved to be hit, and if hurt by the glass, she deserved that too.

At 7 p.m., I received a call from a parent telling me that a drive-by shooter had fired four shots at the school. This happened at about 5:15 p.m. while four or five girls were waiting to be picked up by their parents after basketball practice. We got a description of the car and the person we thought was driving. I went to the high school to talk to our suspect and with the police to search his car. Unfortunately, his car was not there. The police officer warned the suspect that he would be arrested if he came to Jefferson. I called the suspect's mother and asked about the car. Our suspect had beaten up one of our students a few weeks ago.

I was in the lunchroom, handling some discipline issues. My secretary rushed in to get me. There was an emergency in the office. A student's mother was beating her. In the office, I found the counselor between the student and her mother. A very angry mother while yanking her daughter's shirt was screaming in her face. The student was bleeding from her lip where her mother had hit her in the mouth while in their car. I got the mother, the student, and our counselor into my office, but the screaming and anger continued. Finally, the police arrived, arrested the parent, handcuffed her, and hauled her off to jail.

We had an incident at the bus stop after school. A student grabbed a girl's breast after they left the bus. He pulled up her shirt and grabbed her. I had four statements, attesting to the incident. The offender's mother was outraged at me for holding her son accountable. She called my director and the superintendent, claiming that she had gone to the victim's house, and the girl had changed her story. I talked to the victim and her mother. Both said they hadn't changed anything. The offender's mother was simply lying.

A teacher sent a seventh grade girl to the office. She had the imprint of an iron on her face. The imprint of a *hot* iron! It gives me chills to think of it! Her mother hadn't taken her to the doctor presumably because she didn't want anyone to know what she had done. We called the police and DHR. Of the many disturbing incidents I encountered, that was one of the most disturbing. How does a parent get angry enough to take a hot iron and slam it into her child's face? I would say, how does a parent get that out of control? But I see evidence of it on a regular basis.

15

Who Won

"I'm going to kick your fuckin' ass!" she screamed as she came storming off the bus. Sheila may be small, but she was mean as a snake, and she was after a fleeing Jayla.

Sheila had been skipping school when she was caught and brought back by her parents. I put her in class. She wasted no time directing her insolence to her teacher and walking out of class. I stashed her in the library until school was dismissed.

I was supervising as the buses were loading when Jayla came running with Sheila hot on her trail, "I'm going to kick your fuckin' ass!"

I went to intercept Sheila. I got in front of her. She kept trying to push by me, screeching, "Get out of the fuckin' way! Fuck you." I put my arms around her, attempting to contain her. In the meantime, Jayla wisely made herself scarce. I became the recipient of Sheila's anger. She was screaming in my face, trying to wrestle out of my grip while doing her best to knee me.

Students were lined up at the bus windows. Parents were driving by, picking up children. What a spectacle! Sheila, deciding she wasn't going to wrestle free, picked up both her feet, and, overbalanced, we went down in a lump on the ground. I don't even want to imagine what was being said at the sight of us rolling around in the dirt!

A teacher who could have helped, got down on her hands and knees to observe, later claiming she wanted to be able to affirm I had not touched Sheila inappropriately. What the heck! I was more worried about Sheila connecting with one of her knees! That really would have been disastrous. I could have used a little help.

Feeling sweaty and dirty, I finally got Sheila into the office. She screamed and cursed the whole way. With a sigh of relief, I put her in my office and shut the door. The relief was premature as Sheila began systematically dismantling my office. We got her grandmother to pick her up. When her grandmother appeared, Sheila told her to "Fuck off," and stormed out of the building. What a delight that child must have been to parent.

The next morning, I showed up early as usual. I stayed outside, supervising students as they arrived. A sixth grader stopped me as I passed by. He asked innocently, "Dr. Curry, did you win the fight yesterday?" Well, what was there to say to that?

I suspended three boys for jumping another boy. They jumped him because he told on one of their friends for stealing candy. One of the mothers wanted to argue that her son was innocent because the victim didn't see him. The victim didn't see him because he hit the victim from behind. Presumably, the safest place from which to start a fight.

I received a note from a girl reporting a boy for showing off his erection during PE. He gathered a crowd around him so they could all get a good look at his erection through his pants. Apparently, he was quite proud of himself. There was a time that might have been embarrassing. Times definitely have changed.

I was in the hall as school was starting. A teacher poked her head out of her classroom, beckoning me. She whispered, indicating two boys in the back of her room, "They are trying to hide something in their book bag. I think it might be a gun."

I got one of the boys and the book bag out of class, questioning him as we walked down the hall. I was in the process of making sure all the classes were covered. The eighth grader admitted finding something on the track before school.

"Okay. Give it to me!" I said. He reached into the bag and began pulling the object out. All I saw was a pistol grip and thought, *Oh shit. A gun!*

The rest of the object came out of the bag. It was a ceramic-molded penis about a foot long attached to a pistol grip. I hurriedly told him to put it back in his bag. I was relieved it wasn't a gun, but I didn't think it a good idea for him to be out in the hallway armed with a ceramic penis either.

I told him to keep it in his bag, take it to my secretary, close the office door, and give it to her privately. My secretary had a terrific sense of humor. She and the office personnel thoroughly enjoyed showing it off, making jokes, and practicing their quick draw, no doubt. I didn't think the student found it on the track, but I was pretty sure his parents weren't going to claim it.

A teacher stormed in my office. She caught kids stealing her chips from her filing cabinet. One kid admitted it, and one denied it. I took statements from witnesses and suspended them both. I called both mothers. The mother of the kid who admitted stealing the chips worked for the Bessemer board of education. When I called her, she said it was all a setup, and I could not suspend her child. She claimed it was a plot by adults to sabotage the home.

I received this letter from a parent:

> Please excuse Kayla for all of her absences last couple of weeks. We have nowhere to stay right now and she had no running water right now. She is staying with an upstairs neighbor. We don't know if she is going to continue going to Jefferson school when we do find housing.

It was heart rending to read and highlighted, again, the circumstances under which some of our kids lived.

Guns

Taye was lurking between two of our trailers where he had no business when I spotted him. He was nervously holding a purse. I took hold of the purse. He wouldn't let go of it. It was heavy. I insisted on looking in the purse. Taye took off running with me in hot pursuit. I caught him with a much lighter purse. Retracing his route, I found a loaded .38 caliber pistol lying on the stairs.

I called the police, but they wouldn't arrest Taye even though he admitted "finding it in the bushes" because the gun was not on him when I found it. I found that rationale ridiculous.

Apparently, he had somehow been involved in robbing a pizza deliveryman. I don't know what came of that. Taye was a terrific athlete, with a good personality and well liked by other students, although he struggled academically. Sadly, he made very poor decisions, the gun case in point. By eighth grade, Taye had fathered two children by two different girls. He would sit at the lunch table eating. Across from him would be seated the mother of one of his children. As I said, he was well liked. His young parenthood reflected some far greater societal issues as did many other matters, touching the school. Taye was recruited to play football at a private school, but I don't think he could get good enough grades to be eligible to play there.

The eighth grade teachers were concerned about a gun in the building. I searched all the eighth grade lockers. All I found was an XXX rated movie. No gun. The possession of a gun always was a major concern. The possibility of an incident with gang rivalries, personal feuds, and carelessness was ever present. Too many parents did not secure their weapons.

I received a police report stating witnesses saw a black male with a gun on the school grounds. He had opened his coat to show the gun to a group of students. He was not a student at Jefferson and not identified by any witnesses.

A student reported to an eighth grade teacher he saw a gun in another student's book bag. I searched the book bag and found two guns: a derringer and a .25 automatic. No ammunition. The possession of a weapon on school grounds was a sure ticket to the alternative school via a class III hearing.

A student brought a gun to the bus stop. He fired it and pointed it at other students. We were informed of the occurrence by some of the students at the bus stop. We searched him and his friend. We found the gun in his friend's jacket pocket. We called the police and the parents.

Today, I have five class III board hearings. Three hearings are for possession of a gun, one for pushing a teacher, and one for possession of a knife. The first hearing started late due to a father raising cane (rude, yelling) because his daughter was given detention by one of her teachers.

A substitute teacher put Laqueta, a seventh grader, out of her classroom for cursing. Laqueta called her mother. Her mother showed up and walked down to the classroom with a whole group of students ready to verify that Laqueta did not do what she was accused of doing. I intercepted the mother after she had accosted the teacher. The mother denied her daughter ever said that or used that language. I asked the mother to leave and take her daughter with her. I pointed out the teacher had a class and could not have a conference right then. Laqueta's mother started screaming at me. She would not calm down. Her daughter also started screaming. Finally, I had to ask a police officer to escort mother and daughter off the premises. The question of why some of these kids behaved the way they do is no mystery.

One of the eighth grade teachers was out with two stomach ulcers. Her substitute was having trouble controlling the few students in her class. The substitute accused three girls of getting into a fracas. I told the girls to go to the office, intending to sort things out. One of the girls started getting very defensive and yelling, "Fuck you! Fuck you!" to anything I said. She stormed out the door. I called her home but could contact no one. I mailed home a suspension and highlighted a note, saying she could not come to awards night. Sure enough, awards night, she came, trotting across the stage. I felt like saying, *Fuck you, too!* But I avoided a scene and handed her a certificate.

I finally got her mother and a relative in my office. The girl initially lied about the whole incident but finally confessed. Her mother turned on her and vehemently told her with a finger in her face, "I told you never to use those words with the wrong people! I told you never to say that to the wrong people!"

The mother didn't indicate who the right people were.

I came to school and found five trailers broken into. Three trailers had TV, VCR, and typewriters missing. I called the police who fingerprinted several items. As usually happens, I heard nothing more about the break in. Thieves seem to be able to steal from schools with impunity.

We have six sets of twins in the school. Channel 6 came to school today to do a news piece on them.

One of our teachers passed out in the lunchroom. She had a wildly beating heart, asthma, micro valve prolix, and a heart murmur. I called the paramedics and her husband. She was taken to the hospital. After recovering, she was back carrying on at school.

A sixth grader sent a note to our assistant principal saying a boy, Sammy, was harassing her. The assistant principal got Sammy out of class and paddled him. The boy carried on so about being paddled she gave him extra licks. She then went out and got the young lady who sent the note. The young lady told the assistant principal she had paddled the wrong Sammy. That was a really big oops and led to a number of restless nights.

Paddling was an accepted and expected form of punishment in the community. It was a quick consequence for a misdeed. I was not much of a fan. It did not seem to change the behavior of those students most frequently in my office. Ultimately, the Birmingham board of education required written parental permission to paddle and then abolished it all together. Some parents still asked to have their children paddled but that was not an option.

End of term, the assistant principal rewarded a group of students by giving them squirt guns. Squirt guns, for Pete's sake!

She was upstairs handing out squirt guns!

I was downstairs collecting squirt guns!

Middle school students with squirt guns! In school, end of term!

What could she have been thinking!

A student was agitated. She picked fights with at least two other students. She cursed the teacher and other students as she began tearing up folders, overturning student desks as well as the teacher's desk. Totally out of control, she overturned a bookshelf full of teaching materials, tore up a window blind, and kicked in the door, taking it off of its hinges. The police and her mother came on the scene. Her mother tried to restrain her by sitting on her with no success. The police ended up handcuffing her but that didn't prevent her from spitting on anyone nearby. She was a very disturbed young lady in an emotionally conflicted class. Dedicated special education teachers really are special people.

Everyone listened to the verdict on the O. J. Simpson trial. Standing in the hall, I could hear the broadcast from nearby classrooms. The not-guilty verdict was received with very mixed reactions. Cheering from some classrooms, teachers included. Dead silence from others.

Abuse

A police officer came to school to ask about one of our students. The student had a history of sexual abuse by his "uncle." His parents divorced and neither wanted the child. The father gave the child to "Uncle" Phil to raise. The child was sexually abused by "Uncle" Phil and beaten up by his older brother. He ended up with black eyes from his brother and an STD, anal warts, from the "uncle."

When he went to court, the child recanted his story, but the child's history of anal warts was a telling point. He now is living with his stepfather and his mother, and hopefully, "Uncle" Phil is in jail.

We contacted DHR when a student came limping into the office. Her father had beaten her. This is a much-too-common occurrence. We worked closely with DHR. We seldom worked with the same DHR worker. There seemed to be a tremendous turnover in the department. Most of the workers were great, but the turnover hindered consistency.

It is always shocking to me when middle school students get into sex at this early age. This year, we have at least three pregnant eighth graders, one father, and a sixth grader who came to us pregnant.

We had a great home economics teacher who taught a unit on childcare. It emphasized the difficulty in caring for a baby. Initially she used a raw egg that students decorated and had to carry around and care for. The egg was replaced with a doll, a fake baby that students were given to "parent." Each student got to name their "baby" and was given a birth certificate with the baby's name on it. It was a pretty nifty baby doll. It required feeding, diaper changing and attention. It cried when it didn't get what it wanted. It cried at night, demanding the same treatment as a real baby. If the baby was neglected, it cried, and that was recorded for the home economics teacher to grade. The exercise was designed to encourage students to stop and think before they became involved with sex. But, stopping and thinking through actions before committing them is not generally a characteristic of middle school students. Well, to be honest, thinking things through probably is not common at any age where sex gets involved.

We scheduled sex educators to come every year and do a unit with boys and girls separately in seventh grade. The naïve students sat through the course with slightly embarrassed attention. The more street-smart students were ready to fill in any gaps the instructor might have left out.

A student accused her father of abuse. I called DHR and the police. We stayed late at school while the child was interviewed by a DHR worker. The worker found the girl's story credible and issued a pick-up order for her. We waited until a deputy sheriff came out to transport the student to a DHR facility. We were alone in the school by the time the girl left. We made a hasty exit before a very angry, possibly violent, father showed up.

I had a conference with a student, her mother, and a DHR worker. The student had called DHR to report her mother. She spent the weekend in protective custody. According to the mother, an uncle had sexually abused her daughter during the summer.

We had a major disturbance in the lunchroom before school. A female student tried to hit another girl with a metal lunch tray. A third student jumped into the fray. A crowd formed, loving a good fight, and began yelling, jumping up and down, pushing, and surging back and forth. It took three teachers and me to break things up and restore order. The girls were all given class III hearings.

We got word that two of our students' stepfather was killed over the weekend. Their biological father was killed a year ago. I am sure our students will need some grief counseling. School counselors frequently are put in situations they are not adequately trained to undertake. So many bad things happen to kids.

A student came to the assistant principal during lunch period and showed her a letter written by his mother that he found in a notebook. The letter was a suicide letter. Very moving.

> Tony,
>
> This will be the last letter that I write to you. My life seems so worthless. I have tried to please God, you and the kids but I keep on failing. I can't take this heartache and pain anymore. I have tried to hold myself together and pretend that everything is OK. I guess I really am crazy. You didn't respect me and neither did the boys. I deserved the way I was treated. I screwed up. I'm sorry for the hurt or pain I may have caused. My heartache. I wanted you to be happy with me, not ashamed of me. Tell the boys I love them and I'm sorry they were embarrassed of me. Tell my mom I'm sorry and let my family know that I love them. I'm so sorry for everything you will have to face in the next few weeks. Bury me as soon as possible. Spend the least amount of money....

We immediately called the mother to make sure she was alive and notified Officer Malone and DHR. Mother said she was under a doctor's care, and this was one way she relieved stress! I can only imagine the emotions her son felt when he read her letter. So many of the things that come across my desk create terrible burdens for children to carry. And worse, most of these burdens I am helpless to do anything to alleviate.

Coach

The parent loomed over Coach, yelling and screaming. Coach tried to talk to him. The parent's menacing behavior continued. He reached into his pocket for what appeared to be a knife. He was irate because his son had not gotten more playing time in the football game. Coach's attempts to calm him only resulted in more hostility. At the stadium gate, the parent turned on the game officials, ranting and raving at them. Coach made a quick exit. This parent is a perfect example of why students don't learn how to properly handle problems in their lives.

Coach did a great job with our athletic teams. He consistently took a very small turnout in football and turned them into league winners. He did this with basketball and track as well. We also had an excellent girls' basketball coach who literally had her whole team on the honor roll. Our parent turnout at games was very meager. It should be noted, though, that many of our parents held jobs where they were working when other more affluent parents would be off. Many of them were on hourly wages and could not afford to take time off to watch their children play.

Toward the end of the year, Coach organized a staff-student softball game. Coach pitched, and I played shortstop. The fix was in from the beginning. When Coach pitched to the students, he used a ball that they couldn't hit out of the park. He would switch to a standard ball when we were at bat. That gave us a better shot at hitting the ball far enough to pick up a few runs. It was great fun and enjoyed by both students and faculty.

A teacher found a gun in a student's coat pocket, a loaded .25 caliber automatic. The student said it was his stepmother's, and he found it under a trailer at school. It turns out his father was a burglar, and the gun was reported missing from the stepmother's house. Police had records on the father. The student also admitted signing a check he said he found with our counselor's name on it. He said he found the check and several credit cards near his cousin's house. The counselor's purse was taken from a drawer in her office. Driver's license, checks, and credit cards were found along the route to the student's house. The student was arrested.

Larceny was rearing its head at an early age. This may have been a case where a father's influence was not beneficial.

The counselor from Thompson Middle School called to inform me that one of our former students, Tracy, had committed suicide. He had been withdrawn from Jefferson the previous week and enrolled in Thompson Middle School. Apparently, his mother did not want him to continue at Jefferson Middle School, so she sent him to live with his father. Tracy was unhappy both about leaving Jefferson and living with his father.

Tracy got into an argument with his brother, and his father grounded him. Tracy was upset at the punishment. He told his father he was going to kill himself. He went to his room and hanged himself in the closet.

Tracy's mother accosted me as I was leaving his funeral. She said she blamed me for his suicide. I was dumbfounded! I had no idea where that came from! I never had a problem, or even heard of a problem that Tracy might have been having. I am sure Tracy's parents were overwhelmed with grief. I suppose they were looking for some kind of explanation for his death. It left me feeling agitated and profoundly sad.

A student told the assistant principal that his grandfather chased him around with a gun. Our counselor talked to his mother and called DHR. His mother told the counselor that grandfather was always like that. The seventh grader had lived with the other grandparents but taking care of the kids had been too much for them.

His mother said she lives on the street most of the time. Currently, all three have been living on the street in parked cars. His sister skipped school Friday. She left with someone from Jemison and did not return until Sunday night. The mother had no idea who her daughter was with, or where she had been. It really is a miracle that so many of these kids turn out all right with all the obstacles in their lives.

We had a food fight this morning. The majority of one-hundred-plus students in the lunchroom participated.

Most of them are on free or reduced lunch. As a result, I stopped breakfast for Friday. A parent went to my director, so I had to restart breakfast Monday. Sack lunches would be eaten in their rooms for the week. I called out on phone master to notify parents. The incident ended up on the front page of Saturday's Birmingham News. Channels 13 and 42 came out for film and interview.

Groan!

The school was broken into over weekend again. Screens cut in girls' bathroom, glass broken in the door to the library, presumably to reach in and unlock a door. Large-screen TV and VCR were taken. I called the police.

An unknown caller called the school at 10:50 a.m. and stated, "There's a bomb in the building." The caller hung up. The fire bell was rung, and students evacuated the building. The fire and police departments came to the school and found everything to be okay. Students were directed to return to the building.

Two police cars were waiting when I came to work at 6:45 a.m. The school had been broken into, and virtually every TV and VCR were stolen. The second break in within weeks. Glass was knocked out of classroom doors and doors were pried open. The alarm in the hall does not work, and no room with an alarm was bothered. The office door was pried at 5:05 a.m. Sunday. It looked as if someone drove up to the door by the gym. The thieves appeared to have been very familiar with the building. It makes me angry, to say the least, and frustrated. We can't seem to keep anything in our building without it being damaged or stolen.

I received an emergency call from my director saying that a student had been sexually assaulted on the way home yesterday, and her parents were on the way to school. I had a conference with all involved, including the police officer. A police report was filed. The victim, Kayla, said the boy, Dion, asked her to come behind a house to have sex. He unbuckled her pants, pulled them down, and then he exposed himself.

Dion had a different story. He claimed that Kayla asked him to go behind the house to have sex and pulled down her pants. He claimed she exposed him and put his penis into her mouth, but he said no.

Kayla's sister's statement: "Kayla came in the house, threw down her books, sat down, and started crying. I asked her what was wrong, and she said she was scared she was pregnant. She said she swallowed some sperm. She was spitting it out, and he [Dion] turned her head, and it [sperm] went down. Then she said that he stuck it [penis] in her. He got something in his hand and made her lick it."

It was a convoluted story. Neither of these students had a disciplinary record at school. The police sorted it out and worked with both sets of parents for a common agreed-upon resolution.

16

Leah

March 1997

Leah came to us March 1997. She was in kindergarten, a little waif of a child. Pale and emaciated looking, she had metal-capped teeth and a blond stubble for a haircut. Our hearts broke.

Freda and I signed up to be foster parents. We felt there were so many children in need of a good place to live that we could provide a child with a safe, healthy home. In a sense, we felt we were stepping up to the mark, putting actions to our beliefs. Something we were quick to criticize others for not doing. The training required a significant investment of time. Once we were certified, we were able to foster a couple of children for short periods.

Leah's teeth had metal caps due to extensive decaying. Her mother's boyfriend shaved her bead because of reoccurring lice infestations. She had been physically and sexually abused. Her nutrition was appalling. She had scrounged for food and virtually eaten nothing that wasn't out of a can.

We were awakened at night by the sound of Leah roaming around the house, rummaging through our kitchen cabinets. She would squirrel food away in her room. It was a classic symptom of her neglect. We tried to reassure her, to no avail. We put an alarm on her bedroom door so we would know when she got up in the middle of the night. We put locks on all our cabinets, but we continued to find molding and rotten food hidden in her bedroom. It was a very hard habit to break.

Leah struggled in school. It wasn't just her academics, but her behavior that created problems. Academically, Freda worked tirelessly with Leah on her schoolwork. That Leah could competently read was largely due to Freda's diligence. We got Leah a tutor as well. Freda constantly received calls about her poor classroom behavior. It virtually was a daily event. At one point, I enrolled Leah in my school where she had a truly gifted teacher. The next academic year, we were at a loss as to what to do. Eventually, we put her in a nearby school with a principal I knew and a teacher she recommended. Nevertheless, it was another difficult year. Leah qualified for a whole host of special education disabilities. We made sure her individual education plan addressed them. Middle school was a challenge. I enrolled her in a Catholic school nearby. It was expensive, but I felt I had few options. It was hard on Leah. She didn't fit in anywhere. These kids had been together since first grade. Leah was an outsider. On a visit to the school, I saw that someone had drawn a mustache on Leah's class picture. I just did not know what to do with her.

Due to the seriousness of her behavioral issues, Leah was classified a therapeutic foster child. Freda and I saw a DHR-employed psychiatrist on a monthly basis. He endeavored to help us acquire the skills needed to parent Leah. We were struggling. All of the damage, the hurt, and insecurities experienced as a child came boiling up with a vengeance as Leah grew older. The first five years of a person's life have an enormous impact on how a person develops. The trauma of Leah's early years left scars we weren't able to help her overcome no matter how hard we worked.

Our goal was to give Leah as rich and normal childhood as we could. We badgered DHR into getting braces for her teeth and surgery for her scoliosis. They were reluctant but came around. We took her on family vacations and cruises. Our parents became her grandparents. She was in every sense a member of our family. Our child.

But the problems continued. It put an enormous strain on our marriage. Freda thought I was too easy on her. I thought Freda sometimes was too draconian in her attempts to alter Leah's behavior. We were continually in conflict over one thing or another regarding Leah. It all came to a head one afternoon. Leah had been warned about having any open flame in her room. That afternoon, Freda found scorch marks on a wall. That did it for Freda. She was not going to risk Leah burning our house down.

Freda said, "It is me or her! One of us has to go!" When I was slow to answer, Freda turned on her heels, went to our room, packed her bag, and left. That began a period where Freda was living elsewhere, and I was trying to raise Leah on my own. I was overmatched.

Freda and I patched things up, but DHR removed Leah from our home. We stayed in touch with her. Freda worked it out so she could live with us and graduate from the high school where Freda worked. That didn't work because Leah continued to be noncompliant. She simply would not follow any rules, ours or anyone else's. As much as we loved her and wanted to provide her with opportunities for a good life, she seemed bent on destroying it.

I was an inner city school principal, used to dealing with some pretty severe problems, and Freda was a special education teacher, experienced in dealing with difficult children. But neither of us ultimately was prepared to deal with Leah. She simply was too broken.

It was a disheartening ending for us that left us feeling our own inadequacy.

Living elsewhere, she ended up dropping out of high school one course short of graduation. She met some guy online who drove to Alabama and took her back to New York. While she was there, we got a frantic call from the mother of a girl with whom Leah was living. With Leah's help, the girl had gone through her savings. Her mother was dismayed by what was happening to her daughter and the nature of her daughter's relationship with Leah. We did not have any light to share on the situation, but the relationship didn't last, and Leah went elsewhere. When we last heard, she had gotten her GED and was working at a Subway in the state of Washington. Good luck to her.

Gangs

I came from a principals' meeting and ran into a student sobbing. I ask, "What's the problem?"

Taking a breath between sobs, "They slap too hard! I don't want to join!"

"Who are they?" I asked.

As it turned out, she was going to be slapped into a gang. Gangs were a major concern. The Crips, Bloods, and Disciples were the major and violent gangs in the area. At Jefferson, we mostly had wannabe gang members. Wannabe or real made no difference where gang conflict was concerned. If they wore gang colors or hung with gang members, they could be hurt, killed, or intimidated. Gangs didn't differentiate. Parents frequently were in denial and attacked school or police officials for suggesting otherwise. They simply didn't want to hear it.

While I was getting a list of girls in the gang from our reluctant gang novice, three police officers from the gang task force showed up. I asked them to talk with the girls on the list. I sat in the counselor's office, acting in loco parentis as the officers talked to ten different girls. My legal obligation acting in loco parentis was to make sure students' rights were observed and students were neither manhandled nor bullied. One officer went upstairs with the assistant principal to talk with several students. I called all the parents and invited them to a meeting with the police officers, their children, and me the following Friday.

I met with parents, students, and police officers in the lunchroom. The police explained what had happened during their talk with students. I explained what brought it about and the reason for wanting to nip this whole issue in the bud. Ms. Jones claimed the police had threatened and manhandled her daughter during the interview. The officer upstairs with our assistant principal said Alisha had become defiant and loud and that she, the police officer, had restrained her by putting her hands on Alisha's arms and sitting her down. Nothing more forceful happened. Our assistant principal verified that Alisha's behavior was out of control, and the police officer did nothing more than what she described. The police also tried to tell Ms. Jones that Alisha was a key member in this whole gang issue. Ms. Jones was unreceptive, and Alisha was quite insolent to the officer while sitting next to her mother. Apparently, this was another case where the apple didn't fall far from the tree.

We made a serious effort to confront the gang issue. It was an issue to ignore at our peril. The whole gang mentality was dangerous. Jefferson County sheriff's department put out a bulletin about a possible arson attempt at Jefferson Middle School. The bulletin stated the police had "highly reliable" information that the Crips who attend the school were going to burn it as part of the gang initiation.

In another bulletin, the police stated a gang had formed at the high school, calling themselves the RNC (Redneck Crew). It consisted of white males ages fourteen to twenty. They were painting over other gang graffiti in the area, which was perceived as a challenge to that gang, and had talked about burning Jefferson due to the large number of gang members who attended.

Soon after receiving the Sheriff's bulletin, I met with a parent regarding her son's behavior. The student had aggressively confronted a police officer at school. That was a pretty serious deal. The conference included three officers from the gang detail, our counselor, the assistant principal, my director, the parent, stepfather, and me.

The conference started off on the wrong foot and went downhill from there. The parents were late and very hostile. The mother would hear nothing of her son's behavior from me, the police officer, or anyone else. She only came, she said, because she felt coerced with threats of her son's expulsion. She would not listen to anything I had to say, demanding I be excluded from the conference. When the police officer spoke up, she stormed out of the room, slamming the door against the wall. When a member of the gang detail brought up the subject of the student's participation in a gang, the stepfather stormed out of the room. Neither police nor my director could lower the temperature in the room, calm the parents, or steer the conversation to their son's behavior. Whatever the cause for all the hostility the parents were exhibiting, it did not bode well for their son's future.

I never got used to parents not taking responsibility, or allowing their children to take responsibility for their actions. It was a constant reoccurring theme.

When one of our parents went to the assistant superintendent to complain about her child's discipline, I finally got fed up. The following was my reply to the assistant superintendent's inquiry:

> Attached you will find copies of twelve (12) discipline referrals. Please note that eight different teachers wrote them (not counting the P.E. teacher who called her mother but did not write her up). This parent has been contacted by virtually all of this student's teachers. This student had been given before or after school detention, Saturday detention and a suspension. Her mother has been to school for a conference. All of the above has had little impact on the student's poor behavior. The parent knows her daughter's behavior leaves something to be desired, but finds it hard not to want to blame someone else or accept that there are consequences for her daughter's behavior. This is not a new issue.

Mrs. Clark, a straight-laced, very proper, and extremely religious lady was our hearing officer for serious discipline offenses. She'd been in my office and shared her various concerns, including, I might add, the state of my soul. I thanked her for her sincere concern for my spiritual well-being, thinking that no doubt she had good cause. She didn't like to read the profanity that students had used when I wrote a suspension notice describing their behavior. I, of course, took great delight in relating the graphic language students used that got them into trouble. I thought it only fair to share.

We were in a formal hearing with a boy and his mother. The boy had been caught with a girl in a stall in the girls' restroom, his pants around his ankles. Mrs. Clark, talking to the boy, was tactfully trying to get some sense of what actually occurred. She wasn't having much luck with tact. Finally, she got down to brass tacks.

"How close did you come to actually having sexual intercourse?" she asked him.

He looked at her. Thought for a few seconds, held up his hand, thumb and forefinger about a quarter inch apart,

"About this close," he said.

I don't know if that was the response she was looking for, but, stifling a smile, I found it rather enlightening. At any rate, it was case closed in short order.

The morning bell had rung as I rounded the corner and found three eighth grade girls in the hall laughing, carrying on, and making no attempt to get to class.

"Girls, into my office!" I said, pointing at my office door.

Once seated and in my most stentorian tone, I admonished the three for their cavalier attitude in the hall well after they should have been in class. Emphasizing each point, I was up and down in my desk chair, leaning over my desk toward them while giving them my most weighty stare. Finished, with an imperious sweep of my hand, I sent them out of my office.

They were no sooner in the hallway, then they cracked up. I could hear their laughter from my office. Oh! That flew all over me! I charged out into the hallway and hauled them back into my office. Once again, and with much gesturing, I lectured them on their behavior. This time when I sent them to class, I escorted them.

As I returned, my secretary motioned me into my office. She shut the door. With a straight face while looking me in the eye, she pointed down, "Dr. Curry, your fly is unzipped."

I knew I would be the star as students with great delight passed that story around. I decided I would keep a very low profile around school that day. Children can always provide the antidote for taking oneself too seriously.

17

Franklin Elementary

August 1998

"Our students live in those houses," I said. We were standing in front of the school, looking at the unkempt and decaying houses lining the streets. I was talking to a church youth group from an affluent area of town. They volunteered to spend this Saturday working around Franklin Elementary School.

"They get up and go to school every morning like you do. But they come from families that can't give them the support that you get.

"Think about your life, your house, your cars, your vacations, and extracurricular activities. How different would your life be if you weren't born into the family you have?

"You have no control of where and to whom you were born. It is a pure accident of your birth that you have the life that you have.

"I want you to appreciate what you have and to have some empathy for people not as fortunate as you are." It was an important point to make.

After seventeen years at Jefferson Middle School, I was transferred to Franklin Elementary School. We had a new superintendent, and he made wholesale changes. I resented being moved but ended up really liking my new school. Despite all of the various and sundry problems, Jefferson had stayed academically healthy during those seventeen years.

When I got to Franklin Elementary School, it was about seventy-five years old. The inscription over the door said 1925. There was a lot of history. It ran well due to a succession of good principals. Like virtually every Birmingham City school, its demographics had changed. The majority of the student population came from a very low socioeconomic group. About 97 percent were on the free-lunch program. It was one of the first schools in Birmingham to serve the small Latino population. The neighborhood around the school was deteriorating with numerous burned or abandoned houses and many other houses in severe decay. The Latino community largely lived in unkempt blocks of attached houses built during World War II.

Students struggled academically. Many Latino children came from homes where their parents did not speak English or were literate in any language. As a whole, our students seldom had books available at home or parents who modeled reading. Often, their parents had not had successful school experiences. Few were in a position to help their children with schoolwork.

We were able to devote the first two hours of the day to reading with every teacher in the building assigned to help in a classroom. I viewed reading as the primary subject where a student must become proficient. We had some very good teachers. I thoroughly enjoyed sitting in their classrooms, watching them operate. Good teaching, in many ways, is a gift. You can't just punch a time clock and get the job done. Elementary school teachers had the knack for directing, organizing, and motivating their students. It particularly was fascinating to watch kindergarten and first grade teachers. They even had their own language when speaking to their students: "Give me your eyes," to get their students' attention; or wanting them to sit on the rug, "Criss. Cross. Applesauce;" or "Kiss your brains," they would kiss their hand, touch their head, and go; and "*Whoo!*" time to think. Teaching kindergarteners is a lot like herding cats.

We were in a conference in my office. It included my supervisor, the parents, and me. The father, a disheveled, pasty looking man, with a paunch, and hygiene issues, couldn't keep a job. His wife, an overweight, frumpy, bitter woman didn't work either. They just scraped by. They lived in a house with no electricity or water because they had not paid their bill. I contacted a church outreach ministry in order to get their electricity and water turned back on. Over the years, I made sure their son had Christmas presents so he could celebrate like everyone else. This was one of the many conferences regarding their son's behavior. They complained to my supervisor and insisted on a conference including her. The father recited a catalogue of grievances against me none of which included the behavior of his son. It was not atypical for parents to point their finger anywhere other than their child's conduct. Normally I was very restrained in my responses, but it really aggravated me! Truthfully, this conference or any others we held hadn't changed their son's behavior. When I last heard, he continued to be a disruptive force in middle school. It was another example of a child molded by circumstances outside his control in a chaotic home situation with no structure provided by his parents and, at least in his formative years, unable to surmount his environment. It was a common story. The only difference in this story and so many others was there were two parents in the house. Teachers often serve as very positive role models for their students. However, they never can replace the influence of a parent in a child's life. In most cases, the parents' value system becomes their child's value system.

All the fourth graders were sitting along the walls outside their classrooms. "Who remembers the three keys to success?" I asked. I was circulating. Hands would go up. I would pick a student and ask them to name one. Students would name each of the three points. Afterward, I would sum up and elaborate.

"First, show up every day. Whether you are a student or a worker or a father or a mother or whatever. Be there when you are needed.

"Second, always do your best. Always! Never quit. Not just at school but mowing the grass, working a job, being a parent. Be known as that person who always can be counted upon.

"Third, learn to work well with others. There are few things in life you can do successfully on your own. Not in marriage, not in a job, not living in a community. It is not necessarily the most talented who succeeds but he or she who works well with others. For most of us, it takes a team to be successful."

I met with each grade level three or four times each year. I always repeated the same three points. Students got so they could repeat these three points by heart. I hoped that somewhere down the road, they would remember and apply them. I also talked about the importance of their education and how it would influence their life.

"Your education," I told them, "will in many ways determine who you will marry, where you will live, the kind of car you will drive, the house you live in, the vacations you take, and what you will provide for your children. Life is about having some choice in how you want to live. A good education provides you that opportunity." I repeated the same thing at each of these meetings, wanting it to become something of a mantra. I don't know if my talks impacted students, but I always felt better. These three points really are the key to success, and I wanted my students to be successful.

One of our students was a major pain. She utterly defeated all of our efforts to place her in a good learning environment where she could positively direct her energy. She constantly was in trouble. We called her mother regularly. Her mother was partnered with another woman. Both were heavyset, very aggressive toward authority, and unwilling to take any responsibility for the child's behavior.

In reality, I think they felt pretty helpless in dealing with their daughter too. After one particularly frustrating day with the student, I came into the office fussing about the sorry, sorry parent of that sorry, sorry misbehaving kid. My secretary sat stoned faced as I grumbled. She usually did not sit without expression when we talked. Normally, she was quite animated. It slowly dawned on me that someone might be standing behind me. I made a questioning face. My secretary subtly nodded. *Oh! Shit!* Sure enough, there was the child's mother looking as fiercely combative as ever. *Geez*, I thought, *not only is this embarrassing, it could be hazardous!* At that point, I may have been at a loss for words, but the child's mother didn't have that problem.

We had another student who always was met after school by two ladies dressed identically. Their faces were veiled, and they wore black from head to toe. Even on very hot days. With a little careful observation, it became apparent that one of the "ladies" was a male. This went on for over a year. Then one day, only the female appeared. It seemed the man was on the run from the police and went around disguised as a woman. The police finally caught up with him.

A police SWAT team showed up after school in their tactical gear, including assault rifles. Students were gone. They were raiding a house across the street. The third grade classroom overlooking the house was cleared out and a sniper installed at the window. Presumably, it was a drug bust. The raid went smoothly, probably because nobody was home. The ladies that ultimately did get arrested were sisters and parents of several of our students. The students' grandmother was taking care of the children. It was a very common occurrence. A large number of students attending Franklin had relatives in jail, just out of jail, or on drugs. Drugs plagued the community, affecting a great many students' lives. The job of raising children often fell on grandma or auntie. They generally were older, physically limited and with a small financial income. Literally, many grandmothers could not afford to buy the medicine they required to stay reasonably healthy, or have the knowledge necessary to combat their various ailments. For that matter, most couldn't afford the food for a healthy diet to feed their families.

I always found open house interesting. It was the only time we saw some parents. It provided a time for teachers to inform parents and to establish a positive relationship. We had many tattooed parents before tattoos became so popular, mostly women since fathers were seldom in evidence. One mother who always wore a scooped top had B-I-T-C-H tattooed across her chest in large letters: succinct and to the point. I admired the brevity.

I had a morning conference in my office with a fifth grade teacher and a parent. The fifth grade teacher was a very proper middle-aged matron. The parent, a slender woman, came dressed in a short black tight-fitting evening dress with fishnet stockings. This was eight o'clock in the morning. One might suspect she had a very dubious occupation. The conference went well. As we adjourned, I spotted something lying on the floor. Helpfully, I picked it up and immediately switched to holding it with two fingers. It was a pair of small black panties. My fifth grade teacher was aghast! She quickly and vehemently denied they were hers. Well, truthfully, she couldn't have gotten a leg in them. I knew they weren't mine, and we were the only three in the room. The parent disavowed any knowledge of the panties and left. I went straight to the restroom and thoroughly washed my hands.

I was greeting students one morning in front of the school. Shots rang out! *Bam! Bam! Bam! Bam! Bam!* Someone in the motel across the street from the school was blazing away. I thought I was back in Vietnam for a minute. I resisted diving for cover. Previously, three people had been murdered in that hotel. Another person had been murdered at the carwash around the corner. I quickly got all the kids inside the school. The shooting victim was shot five times and survived. The shooter was not found. Amazingly, it was no big thing among our students. For many, it was an all-too-frequent occurrence. Some parents would not let their children out of their house after school. They simply didn't want to take a chance their child would get involved in some of the unsavory activities in the neighborhood.

The kids always seemed to take the brunt of adult's reckless behavior. One of our students was paralyzed. He was collateral damage of an ex-girlfriend trying to shoot the current girlfriend. In another case, a mother came to me for money. Her son had been killed as a result of the drunken mother and her drunken boyfriend driving far too slow in the freeway's left hand lane. Their car had been rear-ended causing it to catch fire. They got out of the car. Her son, sleeping in the back seat, didn't get out. The money, presumably, was for her child's funeral.

18

Retirement

August 2012

I really liked my job. I had an opportunity to work at the board of education, but I liked at least the illusion of being the one responsible for running the school, the school principal. I had a good faculty, an extremely competent rather formidable secretary, and I enjoyed our students, but after thirty-one years, I reluctantly decided to retire. I was seventy-one years old, my school was closing, and all the teachers and students were being reassigned to a new, larger K–8 school. Our school, after almost ninety years, was to be abandoned. Today, it is another sad decaying building in a sad decaying neighborhood. Children's laughter is only an echo of the past.

I ran into a group of teachers in a restaurant who had taught at Jefferson Middle School. They were reminiscing about the good old days. I was surprised when they agreed the best part of their careers occurred while they were teaching at Jefferson Middle School. That was a shock to me. I remember Jefferson as a kaleidoscope of issues, daily tensions, problems, and frustrations with few if any real solutions. It seemed only the students changed. The issues and problems continually reappeared. Of course, they reflected the community.

I admit, I frequently felt like Sisyphus, rolling the stone to the top of the hill only to have it roll down again. This certainly was true at Jefferson Middle School. Despite that, I left education a true believer. I think education is the foundation for everything else. Working in the inner city is hard, and many educators leave it burned out, or angry, or bitter. I fortunately left education with a sense of hope. As many obstacles, hindrances, and challenges that inner city education represents, it still provides an upward path for those willing to take it. I still see America as representing a glowing symbol of opportunity in spite of some of our history or the challenges we face in the present.

The Marine Corps left me feeling I had a big S for Superman on my chest. I could do anything! That certainly wasn't the feeling I had leaving Jefferson Middle School. In retrospect, would I have chosen to go to Jefferson? I would. It had all the elements of adventure and challenge that appealed to me. I worked hard, but I wasn't prepared for so much of what I dealt with to be such an exercise in futility. It seemed to me I continually was swimming upstream against value systems I didn't understand. Franklin was different. I had great empathy for students who came from truly economically depressed circumstances. Race simply wasn't part of the equation. A positive child-centered environment developed, which benefited all of us.

Many of the incidents I have related are just a snapshot of a child's life. They don't tell the whole story. We have no idea of what follows in their lives. Was the abused child able to overcome the abuse to live a normal life? Did the delinquent, or noncompliant and disrespectful child, become a productive, well adjusted citizen? Did I constructively impact the lives of the children in my school? These are questions that hang out there unresolved. They contribute to a slight disquiet carried into retirement.

As teenagers, Gary and I used to cruise Oscars drive-in, checking out the action in his souped-up 1954 Chevy, occasionally revving the engine. Nowadays, Freda and I are more likely to putter around in our golf cart, waving at neighbors on their front porch. Life has slowed. Two artificial hips and a severely arthritic back, no more parachuting. We have gotten old. Well, I've gotten old. I assure Freda she is that same sexy babe who walked into my office all those years ago.

I have been blessed with two great and successful children, now adults with their own families. I have a wife whom I love and who has put up with me for many years. Accumulating money was never a goal in my life. In that, I had great success. I wanted my life to be about contributing to the greater good. I wanted to look back on my life and be able to say it was a meaningful interesting adventure. I accomplished that. It has been.

I was part of history. The Watts Riots, Vietnam, Peace Corps, mobilization for the Gulf War, and desegregation. All had elements of service and adventure. The largest part of my life and energy was spent as part of a team trying to help inner city youth achieve a better life. That was the most dramatic and difficult part where progress was slow and rewards intrinsic.

Teddy Roosevelt said it. "It is not the critic who counts, not the man who points out how the strong man stumbles, or where the doer of deeds could have done them better. The credit belongs to the man who is actually in the arena, whose face is marred by dust and sweat and blood; who strives valiantly; who errs, who comes short again and again; who spends himself in a worthy cause; who, at the best, knows in the end the triumph of high achievement; and who, at the worst, if he fails, at least fails while daring greatly so that his place shall never be with those cold and timid souls who neither know victory nor defeat."

I have lived a life in the arena.

Freda, Adam, Rachel and Mike

Freda and Mike visiting Jamaica for a rugby club reunion

Appendix

Excerpts from 7th Marine Regiment Unit Journal as well as the 1st Reconnaissance Battalion Unit Diary.

7th Marine Regiment Journal
M Co. 3/7

 While moving to obj. 3 rec'd auto. Fire from the N. about 100 meters away. Resulted in one emerg. Medevac. Returned fire with S/A's and 60 mm mortars. Medevac called and completed.

7th Marine Regiment Journal
M Co. 3/7

 Spotted two NVA/VC sitting around bunker. Opened fire with S/A's at approx. 25 meters. Fraged bunkers. Resulted in two NVA/VC KIA, one AK-47, one carbine, documents, medical supplies, one NVA cartridge belt w/canteen and knife, one USMC pack, civilian clothing, 03 NVA helmets, and clothing, 10 lbs of rice, one chicom, five lbs tobacco. Destroyed rice and tobacco.

7th Marine Regiment Journal
M Co., 3/7

 Spotted three NVA/VC opened fire wounded one personnel in ankle. Returned fire swept area with neg. results.

7ᵗʰ Marine Regiment Journal
M Co., 3/7

  While setting in defensive position spotted one NVA/VC standing by stream bed. Advanced on personnel and personnel Chu Hoied. Captured one NVA pack, 20 lbs of rice.

7ᵗʰ Marine Regiment Journal
M Co., 3/7

  Found following articles in bunkers and tunnel complexes: five NVA uniforms, three NVA packs, two 60 mm mortars (complete), one light weight machine gun, five NVA canteens, nine ponchos, five M-16 magazines, one bag of antibiotics, two documents, 13 large cooking pots, eight small cooking pots, one US blanket, one gallon can, one NVA helmet, three yds of gauze, five lbs. dry fish, two RPG rds, one new RPG-2 launcher, two new sighting devices for 60 mm, 110 blasting caps, one small bag DDT poisoning, eight new AK magazines.

7ᵗʰ Marine Regiment Journal
M Co., 3/7

  While searching out hooches personnel came out from behind hooches. Personnel on search party shot before he recognized him as a Marine. Called and completed medevac.

7ᵗʰ Marine Regiment Journal
M Co, 3/7

  Took fire from about 100 meters direct front from S/A's and possible M-16. Returned fire and sent platoon up to reinforce unit. Pulled medevacs back to LZ. Medevac completed. Casualties: 02 WIA.

While on daytime search found the following gear: 1000 lbs of rice, one NVA compass, various books and documents. Destroyed rice and forwarded documents to S-2.

7ᵗʰ Marine Regiment Journal
During the morning of 11 September, Co. K and Co. M moved by truck from LZ Baldy to FSB Ross where Co. K began sweeping toward the battalion from the extreme south. Co. M was helilifted to a blocking position.

Patrol Report for December 7- 17, 1969

Call Sign: Slate Creek/Prime Cut (arty team: Sandhurst)
Composition: 1 Off, 15 Enl, 1 USN – Curry, Elliot, Burns, Rakitte, Clark, Tynes, Boice, Surlock, Comfort, HM3 Prince, Holloway, Green, Wilcutt, Cortez, Grant, Redix, Ailey
Synopsis: 9 sightings of 286 enemy. Team called 7 fire missions resulting in 39 enemy KIA
Observation of Enemy and Terrain:
Dec. 7 at 6:45 p.m. sighted 58 VC/NVA carrying packs, walking trail – F.M. w/neg. clearance
Dec. 9 at 6:17 p.m. sighted 53 VC/NVA carrying heavy packs & rifles on trail – FM neg. clearance
Dec. 11 at 6:22 p.m. sighted 15 VC/NVA wearing dark uniforms and carrying packs on trail. Called FM –excellent coverage observed 1 VC/NVA move from area
Dec.12 at 2:55 p.m. sighted 10 VC/NVA wearing green utilities carrying packs held up in treeline. Called FM excellent coverage resulting in 4 KIA

Dec. 12 at 6:37 p.m. sighted 28 VC/NVA wearing green utilities carrying packs and rifles on trail. Called FM with excellent coverage resulting in 12 KIAs.

Dec. 13 at 6:20 p.m. sighted 60 VC/NVA wearing green utilities carrying packs and rifles on trail. Called FM with excellent coverage resulting in 16 KIAs.

Dec. 13 at 8:20 p.m. sighted 4 VC/NVA wearing green utilities, 2 of the 4 carrying packs along side trail. Called FM with excellent coverage resulting in 4 KIAs.

Dec. 15 at 6:45 p.m. sighted 3 VC/NVA moving east to west and 7 VC/NVA moving west to east all wearing green utilities and carrying packs and rifles. No FM due to larger sighting

Dec. 15 6:50 p.m. sighted 47 VC/NVA wearing green utilities carrying packs and rifles moving on trail. Called FM with good results resulting in 4 KIAs. End of mission due to clouds. Sightings made by Sandhurst

Patrol Report for Jan. 4- 8, 1970

Call Sign: Report Card

Composition: 1 off, 5 enl, 1 USN – Curry, Crowley, Boice, Tynes, Surlock, HM3 Prince, Cortez

Left at 1:43 pm / return Jan 8 at 1:50 pm

Synopsis: Patrol covered a period of 96.5 hours with negative sightings or contacts.

Terrain: generally steep with 12-26 ft. canopy and secondary growth of 6-8 ft. consisting of small shrubs, briar bushes, elephant grass, and vines. Movement difficult and there is water in the area. Good multi CH46 LZ consisting of 4 ft. elephant grass. Freshly broken 2 ft. wide trail made within the last 7 days.

Condition of patrol: fair (team members had emersion feet.)

Patrol Report for January 12 – 26, 1970

Call Sign: Prime Cut (artillery team: Sandhurst)

Composition: 1 off, 17 enl, 1 USN – Curry, Garza, Vaughn, Sigler, Neslon, Ciborowski, Jacqua, Brazington, Hayes, Nottage, Quaid, HM3 Johnson, Redix, Wilcutt, Funke, Kenyon, Lebus, Grant, Schultz

Synopsis: Patrol covered a period of 331 hours with 39 sightings totaling 569 VC/NVA, 2 sightings of 5 caves. Team Sandhurst called 33 fire missions resulting in 61 VC/NVA confirmed KIA. The team utilized 1 spooky with excellent coverage of target.

Observation of Enemy and Terrain:

Jan. 12- 2:35 p.m. Team Sandhurst observed 3 NVA wearing green utilities with negative equipment sitting on a bunker and called FM with excellent coverage of target resulting in 2 confirm KIA

7:15 p.m. Team Sandhurst observed 12 NVA wearing green utilities carrying packs and rifles moving W-E on trail. Called FM with excellent coverage resulting in 6 NVA confirmed KIA.

9:45 p.m. 13 String 18. 13 seismic moving W-E; called 6 rounds HE; movement ceased.

Jan. 13 – 7:40 a.m. Team Sandhurst observed 4 VC/ NVA wearing black P.J.s, green utilities carrying bags, packs and rifles sitting on a bunker. Called FM with excellent coverage resulting in one confirmed KIA.

10:25 a.m. Team Sandhurst observed 1 VC wearing black PJs carrying a pack sitting near a hooch. Called FM with good coverage of target with negative results due to enemy moving out of the area before the first round impacted.

5:45 p.m. Team Sandhurst observed 11 NVA wearing green utilities carrying packs and rifles moving on W-E on trail. Called FM with fair coverage with unobserved results due to darkness.

Jan. 14 – 7:40 a.m. Team Sandhurst observed 20 VC/ NVA wearing black PJs, green utilities carrying packs and rifles going into a bunker. Called FM with excellent coverage of target resulting in 6 confirmed KIAs.

1:30 p.m. Team Sandhurst observed 3 NVA wearing khaki uniforms carrying packs moving into bunker. Called FM with fair coverage of target with unobserved results due to fog setting in.

4:15 p.m. Team Sandhurst observed 2 VC wearing black PJs moving into a bunker. Called FM with excellent coverage of target resulting in bunker being destroyed.

7:00 p.m. Team Sandhurst observed 21 NVA wearing green utilities carrying packs and rifles moving W-E on trail. Called FM with excellent coverage of target resulting in 6 confirmed KIAs.

Jan. 15 – 7:00 p.m. String 18. 4 seismic moving W-E. Called FM 4 rounds HE. Movement ceased.

Jan. 16 – 7:45 a.m. Team Sandhurst observed 2 VC wearing black PJs carrying packs sitting in a bunker. Called FM and gave end of mission due to enemy moving out of the area.

8:45 a.m. Team Sanhurst observed 8 VC/NVA (unable to observe uniforms or equipment due to darkness) moving W-E on trail. Called FM with excellent coverage of target resulting in 4 confirmed KIAs.

Jan. 17 – 6:45 a.m. Team Sandhurst observed 25 VC wearing black PJs carrying packs moving SW-NE on trail. Called FM. Gave end of mission due to time element and enemy moving out of area.

6:45 p.m. Team Sandhurst observed 2 VC/NVA wearing black PJs, green utilities carrying packs and rifles moving NE-SW on trail. Called FM with unobserved results due to fog setting in.

Jan. 18 – 1:00 a.m. Team Sandhurst observed 12 VC wearing black PJs carrying packs and rifles moving NE-SW on trail. Called FM with excellent coverage of target resulting in 9 KIAs.

11:35 p.m. Team Sandhurst observed 6 VC/NVA (unable to observe uniforms or equipment due to darkness) moving NE-SW on trail. Called FM with excellent coverage resulting in 2 confirmed KIAs.

11:38 p.m. Team Sandhurst observed 5 VC/NVA (unable to observe uniforms or equipment due to darkness) moving SW-NE on trail. Called FM and received negative clearance due to friendlies in area.

Jan. 19 – 12:45 p.m. Team observed 2 VC/NVA (1 wearing black PJs, 1 wearing green utilities) carrying packs and rifles. Team observed enemy hide their packs and rifles and changed into white PJs and move NE into village. Team called FM. Gave end of mission due to time element and enemy moving out of area.

1:10 p.m. Team Sandhurst observed 2 NVA wearing green utilities carrying packs and shovels digging a hole behind some brush. Called FM with good coverage with unobserved results due to foliage.

7:10 p.m. Team Sandhurst observed 7 VC/NVA carrying packs and rifles and running W to E on trail. Called FM and got negative results due to friendlies in area.

Jan. 20 – 12:15 a.m. Team Sandhurst observed 5 VC/NVA walking E to W on trail. Called FM with excellent coverage resulting in 3 KIAs.

7:15 a.m. Team Sandhurst observed 12 VC/NVA wearing green utilities and black PJs carrying packs and rifles. Called FM with negative results due to friendlies in the area.

7:10 p.m. Team Sandhurst observed 29 VC/NVA carrying packs and rifles moving W to E on trail. Called FM with excellent coverage resulting in 6 KIAs.

Jan. 21 – 9:05 a.m. Team Sandhurst observed 9 VC/NVA wearing black and white PJs and carrying packs moving E to W on trail. Called FM with fair coverage and unobserved results due to foliage.

7:15 p.m. Team Sandhurst observed 10 VC/NVA wearing green utilities carrying packs and rifles moving W-E on trail. Called FM with good coverage and unobserved results due to vegetation.

8:30 p.m. Team Sandhurst observed 1 VC/NVA (unable to observe uniform or equipment due to darkness) moving

E-W on trail. Called FM with excellent coverage and unobserved results due to vegetation.

8:35 p.m. Team Sandhurst observed 3 VC/NVA (unable to observe uniforms or equipment due to darkness) moving NE-SW on trail. Called FM with excellent coverage with unobserved results due to vegetation.

Jan. 22 – 12:25 a.m. Team Sanhurst observed 16 VC/NVA (unable to observe uniforms or equipment due to darkness) moving E-W on trail. Call FM with excellent coverage resulting in 3 confirmed KIAs.

1:20 a.m. Team Sandhurst observed 3 VC/NVN (unable to observe uniforms or equipment due to darkness) moving E-W on trail. Called FM and gave end of mission due to enemy moving out of the area.

11:55 a.m. Team observed 1 cave 2-3 ft. wide and 10-15 ft. high (team was unable to determine length of cave). Team gassed and threw M-26 grenades into cave with negative results. Cave appeared not to have been used the last 2-3 months

12:35 p.m. Team observed 4 caves 4X5 ft. entrances. Tunnel leading to caves was 3X3. Team gassed and threw M-26 grenades into caves with negative results. Caves appeared not to have been used within the last 2-3 months.

9:10 p.m. Team Sandhurst observed 11 VC/NVA (unable to observe uniforms or equipment due to darkness) moving W-E on trail. Called FM with good coverage of target. Unobserved results due to darkness and vegetation.

Jan. 23 – 3:45 a.m. Team Sandhurst observed 20 VC/NVA (unable to observe uniforms or equipment due to darkness) moving NE-SW on trail. Called FM with excellent coverage resulting in 9 confirmed KIAs.

5:45 a.m. Team Sandhurst observed 8 VC/NVA (unable to see uniforms or equipment due to darkness) moving E-W on trail. Called FM with excellent coverage resulting in 1 confirmed KIA.

7:15 p.m. Team Sandhurst observed 24 VC wearing black PJs carrying packs and rifles moving SW-NE on trail. Called FM and received negative clearance due to save-a-plane. Team utilized spooky with excellent coverage of target with unobserved results due to vegetation.

9:50 p.m. Team Sandhurst observed 4 VC wearing black PJs with negative equipment moving E-W on trail. Called FM and received negative clearance due to save-a-plane.

Jan. 24 – 1:20 a.m. Team Sandhurst observed 2 VC/NVA (unable to observe uniforms or equipment due to darkness) moving W-W on trail. Called FM with poor coverage and negative results.

7:15 p.m. Team Sandhurst observed 8 VC/NVA (unable to observe uniforms or equipment due to vegetation). Called FM and received negative clearance due to save-a-plane.

July 25 – 12:18 a.m. Team Sandhurst observed 8 VC/NVA (unable to see uniforms or equipment due to darkness) moving NE-SW on trail. Called FM and gave end of mission due to enemy moving out of area.

12:45 a.m. Team Sandhurst observed 8 VC/NVA (unable to observe uniforms or equipment due to darkness) moving SW-NE on trail. Called FM with excellent coverage resulting in 3 KIAs.

7:15 p.m. Team Sandhurst observed 61 VC/NVA (unable to observe uniforms or equipment due to darkness) moving

SW-NE on trail. Called FM with excellent coverage with unobserved results due to darkness and vegetation.

8:50 p.m. Team observed 2 VC/NVA (unable to observe uniforms or equipment due to darkness) probing around defensive wire of team's position. Fired 60 mm mortar and team Sandhurst called in defensive FM around the perimeter. Team checked area with negative results.

Jan. 26 – 1:25 a.m. Team Sandhurst observed 5 VC/ NVA (unable to observes uniforms or equipment due to darkness) moving E-W on trail. Called FM with excellent coverage resulting in 1 confirmed KIA.

Patrol Report for January 30- 3 Feb., 1970

Call sign: Report Card

Composition: 1 off, 6 enl – Curry, Garza, Quaid, Nelson, Jordan, Hayes, Brasington

Synopsis: Patrol covered a period of 100 hours with 5 sightings totaling 18 VC/NVA and negative contacts. Team called 1 FM with poor coverage of the target.

Observation of Enemy and Terrain:

Jan. 30 – 4:45 p.m. Team observed 2 VC moving S-N on trail, wearing black PJs and carrying packs. Team took negative action due to enemy moving out of area.

Jan. 31 – 2:00 p.m. Team observed 3 VC moving SE on trail wearing black PJs and carrying packs. Enemy disappeared into brush before team could call FM.

5:50 p.m. Team sighted 2 VC wearing black PJs. Enemy moved to edge of river, picked up 2 large green packs and moved

NE into bushes. Team took negative action because enemy was only visible for 3 minutes.

6:40 p.m. Team observed 8 VC/NVA wearing black PJs, in 3 sampans, moving S-N across river (enemy had packs in boats). Team called FM with poor coverage of target and was unable to observe results due to darkness.

Feb. 2 – 6:05 p.m. Team observed 3 VC/NVA wearing black PJs, in sampan on rivers edge. 1 VC/NVA crossed river W-E, picked up 2 more enemy and went back across river E-W. Team took negative action due to time factor.

Other Information: Insert LZ consisting of a poor, rear wheel zone on a 70 degree slope with hard dirt surface. Best approach into LZ is from the NE. Extract LZ is good 1 CH 46 consisting of 2-4 ft. brush and a hard dirt surface. Best approach into LZ is from the N. Trail running E-W alone ridgeline, 2 ft. wide and presently used.

<u>Conclusions and Recommendations</u>: Patrol leader recommends that patrol be sent into area to monitor trail.

Patrol Report for February 23– March 14, 1970

<u>Call Sign</u>: Sunrise, (arty team was Purple Heart)

Composition: 1 off, 24 enl, 2 USN, k-9 – Curry, Crowley, Jordon, Rakittke, Boice, Tynes, Surlock, Nelson, Quaid, Brasington, Nottage, Vaughen, Cortez, Estes, Kenyon, Grant, Haynes, Funke, Comfort, HM3 Johnson, HM3 Prince, Denson, Wilcutt, K-9 Barron

<u>Synopsis</u>: This patrol covered a period of 441 hours with 25 sightings totaling 236 VC/NVA, and 2 sightings of one

bunker and one base camp. Team Purple Heart (arty team) called 25 FMs with poor coverage of target, resulting in 8 enemy confirmed KIA. Team utilized AO who called a FM with poor coverage of target resulting in 8 enemy KIAs.

Feb. 24 – 3:12 a.m. Team sighted 8 VC/NVA carrying large packs moving E-W on trail. Called FM with good coverage resulting in 1 KIA.

1:30 p.m. Team sighted 2 VC/NVA wearing green utilities moving around camp site. Call FM with negative results due to VC hiding in rocks.

2:10 p.m. Team sighted 1 bunker with suspected movement around bunker. Call FM destroying bunker with a direct hit.

6:15 p.m. Team sighted 1 camp site with tunnel entrance and packs, radios and RPG laying around tunnel entrance. Call FM destroying gear

7:25 p.m. Team sighted 5 VC/NVA moving w-e on trail. Called FM and was cancelled with negative results when enemy ran into bushes.

Feb. 25 – 8:20 a.m. Team sighted 3VC/NVA, 1 female and baby, wearing green and black shirts and green and black shorts near cave. They carried 5 large and 1 skinny packs. Call FM with negative surveillance due to cloud coverage.

8:45 a.m. Team sighted 4 VC/NVA wearing green shirts and black shorts carrying 1 white bag of rice standing in open area. Called FM with negative surveillance due to cloud cover.

10:45 a.m. Team sighted 20 male and 2 female and 3 caves. Men wore green shirts and shorts and women wore light green shorts and bright green sweaters. One was carrying object size of 3.5 rocket launcher, one had SKS, and 2 others were carrying ammo boxes. Called FM with negative surveillance.

7:30 p.m. Team sighted 12 VC/NVA moving W-E. Called FM with outstanding coverage resulting in 5 KIAs.

Feb. 26 – 7:25 p.m. Team sighted 56 VC/NVA walking on trail W-E. Called FM with negative surveillance due to darkness.

Feb. 27 – 7:20 p.m. Team sighted 3 VC?NVA walking W-E along trail. Called FM with negative results due to darkness.

Feb. 28 – 10:30 a.m. Team sighted 1 trail 1.5 to 3 ft wide running NE and used within last week with footprints found on trail.

7:35 p.m. Team sighted 5 VC/NVA walking W-E. Called FM with excellent coverage and negative surveillance due to darkness.

Mar. 1 – 8:00 p.m. Team sighted 2 VC/NVA standing on trail. Called FM with excellent coverage and negative surveillance due to darkness.

Mar. 2 – 1:15 p.m. Team sighted 2 VC/NVA wearing black PJs sitting in hooch. Called FM with negative surveillance because NVA left area and due to terrain.

Mar. 3 – 9:50 a.m. Team sighted 4 NVA wearing white shorts, shirts carrying timbers and shovels walking along trail W-E. Called FM with negative results because enemy left position.

Mar. 4 – 7:05 p.m. Team sighted 4 VC/NVA wearing black PJs and carrying packs walking W on trail. Called FM with negative surveillance due to darkness

Mar. 5 – 6:25 a.m. Team sighted 6 VC/NVA walking NE-SW in rice paddies. Called FM with negative results due to darkness and terrain.

7:00 p.m. Team sighted 3 VC/NVA walking W-E on trail. Called FM with negative clearance due to save-a-plane.

Mar. 6 – 7:10 p.m. Team sighted 5 VC/NVA heavily camouflaged with trees and branches carrying packs walking W-E on trail. Called FM with negative surveillance due to darkness.

Mar. 8 – 7:22 p.m. Team sighted 40 VC/NVA walking W-E on trail. Called FM with excellent coverage and negative surveillance due to darkness.

Mar. 9 - 7:30 p.m. Team sighted 30 VC/NVA walking W-E on trail. Called FM with good coverage and negative surveillance due to darkness.

Mar. 12 – 7:45 p.m. Team sighted 5 VC/NVA carrying packs walking W-E on trail. Called FM with good coverage and negative surveillance due to fog.

Patrol Report for March 18, 1970 – Mar. 22

Call Sign – Pony Boy

Composition: 1 off, 5 enl, 1 USN - Curry, HM3 Johnson, Cortez, Jaqua, Brasington, Ciborowski, Vaughan

Synopsis: This patrol covered a period of 97 hours with negative sightings and contacts.

Terrain: Generally rolling with 60-90 ft. canopy and secondary growth 6-12 ft. consisting of vines, small bushes, bamboo, elephant grass, thorns, thick bushes. Difficult movement

50-75 meters per hour. There was water in area not seasonal and in low areas.

Patrol Report for March 25 – April 1, 1970

Call Sign: Patty Shell

Composition: 1 off, 6 enl – Curry, Grant, Nelson, Hayes, Nottage, Sigler, Quaid

Synopsis: 6 sightings of 17 VC/NVA, 1 base camp, comm. wire, sleeping platform, 2 caves, footprints, and 1 harbor site, negative fire missions

Observation of Enemy and Terrain:

Mar. 25 – 12:30 p.m. Team sighted natural rock formation with 2 man sleeping platform underneath constructed of bamboo measuring 4X5 ft. and old area had been previously bombed and platform not used in 3-4 months. Area provided good natural canopy/cover and was not visible from the air.

4:45 p.m. Team sighted 2 caves, 1 measuring 6 ft. high, 15 ft. deep and 10 ft. wide capable of holding 3 men. Caves consisted of natural rock formations on side of hill and were not man made. Caves were reinforced with bamboo poles and appeared to have been used by the enemy at one time but were recently used by friendly infantry due to the team discovering ration cans, 1 plastic canteen and 1 demolition kit bag laying around the area.

March 28 – 12:30 p.m. Team sighted 1 base camp measuring 125X100 meters consisting of 9 hooches with hospital and mess hall, 7 bunkers, 3 storage/fighting holes, 2 rifles and numerous documents and gear. First area measuring 30X40 ft.

consisting of 4 hooches measuring 12X30 ft. and constructed of bamboo thatched together with twine and 3 bunkers measuring 6X20X6 ft. Bunkers were situated under hooches and hooches were spaced 15-30 ft apart. First base camp area had not been recently used. Second area of base camp measured 100X50 ft. and consisted of 3 hooches measuring 12X30 ft. and constructed of bamboo thatched together with twine and 4 bunkers situated under hooches measuring 6X20X6 ft. All bunkers in the base camp areas were dug under hooches and reinforced with bamboo poles along walls. Second area also had 1 hospital and 1 mess hall both measuring 20X30 ft. and constructed of bamboo. Mess hall contained tables measuring 6X3 ft. with plates on them and freshly cooked rice in pot and 2 plates that had recently been eaten out of. Hospital contained numerous bottles of medicine, numerous documents, assorted clothes, 1 SKS rifle and 1 bolt action rifle, both rusty. Mess hall and hospital were both capable of holding 25-30 men. Second base area also had 3 storage/fighting holes measuring 5X5X5 ft., 2 transistor radios with parts missing, 4 large rectangular shaped batteries measuring 6X3 inches and taped together and 2 NVA type canteens. Team also sighted in second base area 3 fresh piles of human defecation and 1 fresh set of footprints heading east. Base areas were approximately 50-75 meters apart. Team took negative action due to lack of communication and moved out of the area. Team believed the enemy was reoccupying the second base camp area. Team took documents, rifles, samples of medicine and canteens with them.

5:30 p.m. Team sighted comm. wire running parallel to trail SW-NE. Comm wire was situated 5 ft off the trail on NE side. Team also sighted C ration cans lying around area and believe infantry may have been in the area. Team followed comm. wire for 25 meters and cut wire.

Mar. 30 – 11:00 a.m. Team sighted 2 sets of fresh footprints heading SW on hard packed trail and 1 harbor site, recently used and large enough for 4-5 men situated off trail.

1:30 p.m. Team sighted 17 VC/NVA wearing green utilities and mixed PJs carrying 16 large packs and at least 5 rifles. Point man wore green shorts, green utility shirt and NVA helmet and carried an AK-47. Enemy group consisted of men and women. Enemy was moving S, 50 meters NW of team's position. Team took negative action due to lack of communications. Team moved out of the area to ridgeline and establish communications and called AO. AO came on station but could not relocate the enemy position.

Terrain: Area was generally rolling to steep with 15-25 ft. single canopy and secondary growth of 4-6 ft. consisting of vines, small bushes, bamboo, boulders, thorn and thick bushes. Movement within patrol area was moderate averaging 200 meters per hour for a recon patrol. Water was plentiful in the area.

Patrol Report for April 7-11, 1970

Call Sign: Pony Boy
Composition: 1 off, 6 enl, 1 USN, 2 ARVN
Curry, Hayes, Quaid, Hoe, Nelson, Doc. Johnson, Sgt. Garza, Hai

Synopsis: This patrol covered a period of 97.5 hours with 3 sightings of fighting holes. Team had negative contact.

Judging from the fighting holes and c rat cans, the area appeared to have been occupied by our infantry

Observation of Enemy and Terrain:

April 8 – 4:55 p.m. Team sighted 2 fighting holes 4X5X3 able to hold 4 men and were approximately 1 year old. "C" ration cans were around the fighting holes

April 9 – 9:00 a.m. Team sighted 2 fighting positions with bunkers. Burnkers were 5X5 ft. and were very old, capable of holding 3 people and were camouflaged with elephant grass. Bunkers were not built good and haven't been used recently.

9:00 a.m. Team observed 10 infantry fighting holes. Each fighting hole was built for 2 people, measuring 2X3X3 ft. and were covered by overgrown elephant grass. "C" rations and assorted gear were found in area being approximately 3-4 months old.

Terrain: Generally rolling to steep with 20 ft. canopy and secondary growth of 4-5 ft. consisting of elephant grass. Movement easy averaging 300-400 meters per hour for a recon patrol.

Patrol Report for April 12 – 26, 1970

Call Sign: Sunrise (arty team: Nigeria)

Composition: 1 off, 21 enl, 2 USN – Curry, Garza, Jordan, Boice, Tynes, Kenyon, Comfort, Manela, HM3 Prince, Grant, Quaid, Nelson, Wilcutt, Nottage, Sigler, Hayes, Surlock, West,

Sierra, Brasington, Vaughn, Jaqua, HM3 Johnson, Dissinger, Cortez

Synopsis: This patrol covered a period of 331.5 hours with 6 sightings of 53 VC/NVA. Team Nigeria called 3 FM with good coverage of target but unobserved results due to terrain.

Observation of Enemy and Terrain:

April 13 – 6:40 p.m. Team Nigeria sighted 10 VC/NVA wearing mixed utilities carrying heavy packs and rifles moving E toward village. Called FM but received negative clearance.

April 15 – 9:15 p.m. Team Nigeria sighted 5 VC/NVA moving up hill toward team's position. Sunrise also made sighting and fired 60mm mortar. Nigeria called FM with excellent coverage but unobserved results due to terrain.

April 18 – 6:30 p.m. Team Nigeria sighted 6 VC/NVA wearing green utilities carrying heavy packs and rifles walking N on trail toward village. Called FM but received negative clearance.

April 19 – 12:15 p.m. Team Nigeria sighted 4 VC wearing black PJs building a hooch. Called FM with poor coverage.

7:50 p.m. Team Nigeria sighted 25 enemy carrying packs and rifles moving W on trail. Called FM with good coverage but unobserved results due to darkness.

April 22 – 3:20 p.m. Team Nigeria sighted 2 VC wearing black PJs carrying rifles and 1 light machine gun following stream bed S. Sunrise also made sighting and fired on enemy position with 50 cal. machine gun resulting in enemy fleeing the area.

Patrol Report for May 5 – 9

Call Sign: Veal Stew

Composition: 1 off., 6 enl. Curry, Brazington, Sierra, Jaqua, Redix, Tomalin, Vaughn

Synopsis: This patrol covered a period of 96.5 hours with negative sightings and negative contacts with the enemy.

Observation of Enemy and Terrain:

May 5 – 4:25 p.m. Team observed smoke and heard 5-6 rocket blasts being ignited approximately 1000-1500 meters to the W-SW of teams position. Team called radio-relay who called FM and AO, team could not observe results due to distance and denseness of canopy

May 7 – 4:00 p.m. Team heard a single rifle shot approximately 1500 meters to the SW of teams position.

6:45 p.m. Team heard a sound of 2 rockets being launched in the valley. Team could not observe flashes or smoke due to denseness of canopy. Team did not call FM as a result of comm. failure (radio relay went down)

May 8 – 3:45 p.m. Team heard 3 rifle shots with an interval of one minute between 1st and 2nd rounds and approximately 5 minutes between 2nd and 3rd shots.

4:05 p.m. Team heard three rifle shots at 30 minute intervals

Terrain: Generally steep with 60 to 100 ft. canopy and secondary growth of 2-6 ft. consisting of vines, small bushes, bamboo, elephant grass, thorns, thick bushes. Movement within the patrol area was difficult averaging 75-100 meters per hour for a recon patrol. Water was in the high and low ground and was not seasonal. Animal life consisted of snakes, squirrels, rock apes, birds, and rodents.

Team received scattered small arms fire from the E as they were being extracted.

Patrol Report for May 14 – 17, 1970

Call Sign: Thin Man

Composition: 1 off, 5 enl, 1 USN - Curry, Cortez, Hayes, HM3 Prince, Grant, Shieffield, Dissinger

Synopsis: This patrol covered a period of 73 hours with negative sightings or contacts.

Terrain: Steep with 50-6- ft. canopy and secondary growth of 5-6 ft. consisting of vines, small bushes, bamboo, boulders. Movement difficult averaging 50-75 meters per hour for a recon patrol. There was no water in the area. Animal life consisted of birds and snakes.

Used radio relay: X-Ray

Patrol Report for May 24-26, 1970

Call Sign: Veal Stew

Mission: Secure LZ for 7th Marines

Composition: 1 off, 5 enl, 1 USN - Curry, Jacques, Clark, Gates, DeLoach, Weaver, HM3 Beck

Synopsis: This patrol covered a period of 49 hours with negative sightings but one incident of hearing an estimated

4-5 enemy breaking brush and negative contacts with the enemy. Team utilized supporting arms of AO.

Observation of Enemy and Terrain:

May 25 - 6:30 a.m. Team was in harbor site when they heard movement in the bush moving E-W approximately 50 meters S of team's position. Team estimated 4-5 enemy were moving through the area. Team moved out of harbor site to the high ground and called an AO. AO came on station and delivered his ordnance on the target area with excellent coverage but unknown results due to negative observation.

Terrain: no canopy, secondary growth consisting of vines, small bushes, boulders, thorns and high bushes.

Conclusion: 2 days too long a period for securing an LZ as team was forced to evade for the duration of the patrol. Recommend 1 day at the most for securing an LZ for the infantry when team is inserted into the same LZ.

Patrol Report for June 8, 1970

Call Sign: Fast Day

Composition: 1 off, 3 enl, 1 USN, 2 ROKMC

Synopsis: This patrol covered a period of 6:20 hours with negative sightings and 1 SFD incident.

Observation of Enemy and Terrain:

June 8 -10:00 a.m. Team moved on trail along ridgeline to the NW. Trail was 2 ft. wide and not recently used. The area is completely bombed out negative canopy and under growth.

3:00 p.m. Team began to move on trail when Sgt. Crawford stepped on pressure type SFD resulting in his blow-

ing the forward section of his left foot off, leaving only his heel. The hole discovered after detonation was 1.5 ft. around and 6 inches deep. No black burned areas. (Patrol Leader believes possible toe popper M-14 US type). Patrol Leader requested Medevac and AO/gunship coverage. Corpsman gave first aid to WIA. Gunship on station 1515H. Medevac arrived on station and completed 1530H.

3:30 p.m. Team moved to insert LZ and was extracted at 1620H.

Terrain: Steep to rolling negative canopy and secondary growth consisting of vines, boulders, area completely bombed out, dead fall everywhere. Movement within patrol area was easy averaging 300 meters an hour for a recon patrol.

Conclusions and Recommendations: Team found some black clothes and some wrapping paper used to wrap gauze bandages. It has been noted with concern by the Patrol Leader that the last 5 times out the WP grenade's safety levers have been breaking off. Patrol Leader indicates he was unable to move in this area undetected.

Patrol Report for June 10-13

Call Sign: Fast Day
Composition: 1 off, 4 enl, 1 USN, 1 ROKMC -
Curry, Cottrell, OFarrell, Gonzalez, Stamper, HM2 Preston, Kim
Synopsis: This patrol covered a period of 66.5 hours with negative sighting and negative contacts with the enemy.

Terrain: Rolling to steep with 60 ft. canopy and secondary growth of 8-10 ft. consisting of vines, small bushes, bamboo, elephant grass, boulders, thorns, thick bushes. Moderate to difficult movement. Water in low ground, not seasonal. Animal life consisting of deer, squirrels, leeches, rock apes and birds.

Patrol Report for June 18-22, 1970

Call Sign: Turf Club

Composition: 1 off, 6 enl. Curry, Thompson, Jordan, Redix, Kenyon, Funke, Mathern

Synopsis: This patrol covered a period of 99 hours with negative sightings and negative contacts with the enemy.

Terrain: Razor back

Condition of Patrol: generally good but wet

Recommendations: Past recon teams have not been policing up harbor sites prior to departing. Suggest strong action be taken to ensure this is corrected so that the position of future patrols is not compromised.

Patrol Report for June 25-28, 1970

Call Sign: Report Card

Composition: 1 off, 5 enl, 1 USN Curry, Thompson, Bumpe, Funke, Gates, Mathern, HM3 Prince

Synopsis: This patrol covered a period of 78 hours with negative sightings and negative contacts with the enemy.

Terrain: Generally steep with 50-70 ft. canopy and secondary growth 3-6 ft. consisting of vines, small bushes, bam-

boo, elephant grass, boulders, thorns, thick bushes. Movement was difficult. Water in low ground not seasonal. Animal life: rock apes, boars, monkeys, leeches, insects. Insert LZ was good one helo LZ measuring 60X40 meters consisting of high shrubs and elephant grass. Best approach to the LZ is from the E or W. Extract LZ was good 1 helo LZ measuring 100X60 meters consisting of high shrubs and elephant grass. Best approach is from the S. A trail 2 ft. wide running N-S was recently used.

Patrol Report for July 13-17, 1970

Call Sign: Moon Dash

Composition: 1 off, 4 enl, 1 USN, 1 ROKMC Curry, Nelson, Haynes, HN West, Jordan, Brunelle, Chung

Synopsis: This patrol covered a period of 102 hours with 2 sightings of 1 trail and 3 fighting holes (reinforced with 3 inch diameter logs and 4 inches of dirt). Negative contacts with enemy.

Terrain: Steep with negative canopy and secondary growth 4-6 inches consisting of small bushes and thick bushes. Easy movement. Insert LZ was "Sunrise" hill 425. Extract LZ a good one helo, 4ft. elephant grass. One foot wide trail used in the last month.

A resupply helicopter leaving Hill 425. Note the tower with the IOD.
It assisted in targeting NVA movement in the Que Son Valley.

On patrol opening a can of c-rats, probably peaches, which
along with pound cake were a universal favorite.

About the Author

Mike Curry grew up in San Diego, California. After five years in the National Guard, including mobilization for the 1965 Watts Riot, he joined the United States Marine Corps. He served a tour in Vietnam as an infantry officer, mainly leading long-range reconnaissance teams. Following the Marine Corps, he volunteered for the Peace Corps and was sent to Jamaica, where he lived for six years. During that time he consistently was selected to represent Jamaica on their National Rugby Team. Returning to the United States, he earned a PhD at the University of Alabama and spent the next thirty-one years as a principal of an inner city school in the Birmingham City School System during a time of court-ordered desegregation. He joined the 20th Special Forces Group and went to Jump School at age forty-nine. Currently retired, he is married with two children and four grandchildren.